Power, Labor, and Livelihood

Power, Labor, and Livelihood

Processes of Change in Rural Java

GILLIAN HART

UNIVERSITY OF CALIFORNIA PRESS
Berkeley   Los Angeles   London

University of California Press
Berkeley and Los Angeles, California

University of California Press, Ltd.
London, England

© 1986 by
The Regents of the University of California

Printed in the United States of America

1 2 3 4 5 6 7 8 9

Library of Congress Cataloging in Publication Data

Hart, Gillian Patricia.
Power, labor, and livelihood.

Bibliography: p.
Includes index.
1. Agricultural laborers—Indonesia—Jawa Tengah.
2. Income distribution—Indonesia—Jawa Tengah.
3. Jawa Tengah (Indonesia)—Rural conditions. I. Title.
HD1537.I56H37   1986   330.9598'2   85-8435
ISBN 0-520-05499-7 (alk. paper)

To my parents

Contents

Tables

Illustrations

Preface

This book represents a prolonged effort to comprehend and interpret some of the changes taking place in Javanese rural society. It originates from dissertation fieldwork that I conducted (in 1975–1976), in a Central Javanese village that I shall call Sukodono, and has been stimulated by a series of more recent controversies over the nature and causes of agrarian change in Java. In the transition from the original fieldwork to the completion of this book, my approach to understanding agrarian problems has itself been radically transformed.

I went to Java in 1975 equipped with two sets of conceptual baggage: an econometric model designed to estimate labor supply functions, and a view of Javanese rural society derived from Clifford Geertz's *Agricultural Involution* (1963). Both of these soon disintegrated. My initial plan to gather data from a number of different villages in order to ensure both statistical representativeness and variation collapsed when I realized that I would be fortunate merely to scratch the surface of what was happening in a single village. Not only did my methodology change, but so too did the questions that I was asking. It soon became evident that, contrary to Geertz's notion of shared poverty, apparently small differences in landholdings were associated with wide differences both in the ways in which men, women, and children went about earning a livelihood and in their positions in rural society. I therefore shifted the focus of the dissertation to examine how and why labor and resource allocation varied among asset groups. One of my chief findings was that the differences in access to agricultural wage labor formed a key part of the explanation of interhousehold differences in allocative behavior (Hart 1978).

The general importance of these findings became increasingly evident after 1978 when large quantities of national data on trends in employment and income distribution in rural Java over the first half of the 1970s became available. The interpretation of these data proved highly ambiguous; instead of clarifying what had been happening to different groups, the data provoked tremendous controversy over whether or not poor rural Javanese had benefitted from rapid economic growth.

The immediate issue at stake in this controversy—whether or not rural labor markets operate competitively—is similar to that which arose in my fieldwork. Underlying this debate is the broader and equally contentious question of the nature and causes of structural change in rural Java.

This question is extremely important. Rural Java is the most densely populated agrarian economy on earth and the locus of some of the world's most extreme poverty. The fate of different rural groups over the first part of the 1970s assumes added significance in view of the massive political and economic changes in Indonesia since the late 1960s. During the first half of the 1960s, the Indonesian Communist party (PKI), the second largest in Asia, was actively engaged in a strategy of mobilizing the poor Javanese peasantry in order to strengthen its power at the center. These efforts culminated in the abortive coup of September 1965 in which the PKI was accused of assassinating six Indonesian army generals, and were followed by agrarian massacres in which many hundreds of thousands of actual and alleged PKI supporters in the Javanese countryside were slaughtered or imprisoned. In 1966 the New Order regime under General Suharto took power and instituted far-reaching political and economic changes that involved the suppression of most forms of political activity and a heavy emphasis on economic stabilization and growth. These changes were supported by the resumption of Western aid on a large scale and accompanied by substantial inflows of foreign capital. Indonesia's position as an oil exporter meant that rapid economic growth was further bolstered by the escalation of oil prices from late 1973 onward. The accession to power of the New Order also coincided with the availability of chemical-biological advances in rice production, which were widely disseminated in the countryside of Java.

This background of profound political, economic, and technological change lends added importance and complexity to the question of what has been happening in rural Java and its causes. Addressing both the macro data controversy and the debate over the nature of agrarian change in Java, I shall draw on the insights that have grown out of the Sukodono study in an effort to shed light on the processes of structural transformation.

The transition from my original study to the completion of this book has involved trying to understand the ways in which local processes are both shaped by and act on wider political-economic forces. The title of the book—*Power, Labor, and Livelihood*—signifies the three main levels of analysis that constitute the conceptual framework. Working within this multilevel framework, I have sought to identify how the different levels are connected with one another and to explore some of the agrarian consequences of declining oil revenues in the context of future processes of state formation.

In writing this book, I have incurred substantial intellectual debts to a number of people and received extensive institutional and financial support from a variety of sources. The original fieldwork was conducted in affiliation with the Indonesian Agro-Economic Survey. It was made possible by Rudolf Sinaga, William Collier, and Achmad Birowo together with the Lembaga Ilmu Penelitian Indonesia, and supported by the Social Science Research Council, the Agricultural Development Council, and a grant from the Agency for International Development to Cornell University. Subsequent fellowships from the International Labor Organization and Radcliffe's Bunting Institute released me from teaching and administrative duties, and the Bunting Institute provided me with the tranquil and supportive environment that I needed to complete the book. My first and most lasting intellectual debt is to John Mellor whose work on rural labor allocation in the early 1960s stimulated my interest in the topic and who consistently encouraged and contributed to the dissertation and to the evolution of this book. The other members of my dissertation committee at Cornell University—Daniel Sisler, Timothy Mount, and Norman Uphoff—also have my enduring gratitude. Another early and ongoing source of inspiration is Benjamin White whose approach to the analysis of Indonesian society, along with those of Benedict Anderson and Sajogyo, have heavily influenced my own.

Sara Berry, Peter Doeringer, and Theresa Flaim have combined stern but constructive criticism with unflagging support through many drafts of the manuscript. I have also benefitted tremendously from critical readings by John Bowen, David Dapice, Howard Dick, Susan Eckstein, Michael Lipton, Gustav Papanek, Paul Streeten, and Lance Taylor, and from discussions with Steven Stoft. Barbara Metcalf and Daniel Lev made important contributions in the later stages.

Marla Richmond undertook the complex task of assembling the final manuscript and preventing the word-processing system from devouring it, and I am extremely grateful to her.

To my parents, who stood by me through the many ups and downs that have led to its completion, this book is dedicated.

1
INTRODUCTION

Few countries in recent history have experienced political and economic change on a scale comparable to that of Indonesia. Since its accession in 1967, the New Order regime has brought about a dramatic transformation of the entire political-economic system within the preexisting structure of heavily centralized state power. Massive inflows of oil revenues after 1973 have reinforced state control and drawn Indonesia more tightly into the global economy.

Evaluations of the New Order differ widely. Some observers point to the government's success in restoring stability in the wake of the extreme political and economic chaos of the late Sukarno era and in generating rapid growth. Others stress the growing concentration of wealth, the widening rural-urban disparities, and the authoritarian structures within which growth and stabilization have been achieved. Most agree, however, that Indonesia's future hinges on the fate of the Javanese peasantry who form the majority of Indonesians and who are crammed into the most densely populated rural area on earth.

This book is an inquiry into what has been happening in rural Java and its causes. At the core of this inquiry is the way in which the men, women, and children of Sukodono (a pseudonym for a rice-cultivating village in north-Central Java) attempt to secure their livelihood. I shall attempt to identify the forces that shape the labor strategies of different households and to explore the consequences of the villagers' efforts to adapt to and manipulate the networks of social relations that define their access to work and income.

The analysis of rural labor and livelihood is cast within the specific context of the larger political-economic system and focuses on understanding how macro forces both influence and are influenced by what happens at the local level. In particular, the methods that employers use to recruit and discipline labor are linked with wider political and economic forces, as well as with the livelihood strategies of different households. By elucidating the connections among these three levels, I shall show how the pattern of agrarian differentiation in Sukodono is part of a larger process of structural change that involves major shifts in the state's interests in and relations with the rural sector.

The analysis that grows out of the Sukodono study has a direct bearing on two major controversies over the causes and consequences of agrarian change in Java. One debate concerns the interpretation of macro data on trends in rural employment and income distribution in the 1970s, in particular, the question of whether labor was being pushed or pulled out of agriculture. A related and similarly controversial set of issues is the nature and causes of the structural transformation of Javanese rural society. Participants in this debate agree that the main engines of agrarian change are population growth along with modern rice production technology and the commercialization that it engenders, but they differ in their analyses of how these variables operate.

My approach in this book sheds light on these controversies in two related ways. First, I analyze some important mechanisms of rural labor arrangements, which facilitate interpretation of the macro data before and after the late 1970s. Second, my focus on the ways in which local-level processes both reflect and alter larger political-economic forces helps resolve the problems encountered by students of agrarian change who base their theories primarily on demography and technologically induced commercialization. Although specifically concerned with Java, I seek to illustrate a general approach to the understanding of agrarian differentiation and class formation.

AGRARIAN CHANGE IN JAVA: ISSUES AND CONTROVERSIES

The Macro Data Debate

The macro data debate stems from the ambiguity of census and national survey data on trends in employment and income distribution. These data show a consistent decline in the proportion of the work force employed in agriculture and remarkably little rural-urban migration over much of the 1970s, but they contain virtually no direct evidence of the rural nonagricultural activities that seem to have expanded so rapidly in this period. One possibility is that rural Javanese were being enticed out of rice agriculture by more lucrative opportunities in occupations stimulated by buoyant economic growth or that these activities at least expanded sufficiently rapidly to prevent declining incomes. Alternatively, the data could reflect a process of marginalization whereby people were being driven into peripheral activities in order to survive. The national survey data on trends in levels of living over the first part of the 1970s are similarly ambiguous. Depending on the method used to correct for the effects of inflation, one can conclude that either the poorest 40 percent of the rural population on Java enjoyed increases in real income of about 4 percent per year or that their real incomes on the average declined.

Whether labor markets operate competitively has become the central issue in the debate over interpretation of the national-level data on employment and levels of living over the first part of the 1970s. Those who argue that people were being induced rather than pushed out of agriculture assume that rural labor markets tend toward a competitive norm and conclude that the returns to labor in nonagricultural activities must more or less have approximated those in agriculture. Hence their contention that "despite the relative decline in the demand for labor in Javanese agriculture and the displacements associated with structural changes in agricultural technology and institutions, the demand for labor in non-agricultural activities appears to have expanded sufficiently to avoid any general and substantial decline in real wages in Java" and that "the rise in labor force participation rates is most reasonably interpreted as a response to the expansion of employment opportunities and a mechanism through which the work force has been able to participate in rising levels of national income" (Leiserson et al. 1978: 45, iii).

The alternative view is that Javanese rural labor markets are divided into "formal" (rice) and "informal" (nonrice) sectors, with lower returns to labor in the informal sector (Lluch and

Mazumdar 1981). This notion of labor market structure offers a rationale as to why growth in the economy as a whole could have been accompanied by a process of marginalization but fails to explain why these barriers emerge and disappear or whether they can be expected to occur in some circumstances, but not in others.

My analysis of rural labor arrangements also supports the pessimistic interpretation of trends in employment and income distribution over the first part of the 1970s. By viewing worker-employer relations within the context of wider political-economic structures rather than as isolated and static micro phenomena, it helps explain variations and changes in institutional arrangements.

Changes in labor arrangements in Java have been particularly dramatic since the late 1960s and have assumed the form of restrictions on access to rice-harvesting jobs as well as to pre-harvest jobs.[1] The open harvest, in which all who wish to participate are paid a share of the paddy they reap, is usually regarded as the archetypal Javanese "poverty-sharing" institution.[2] Accordingly, the explanation of these changes is of major importance and forms the focus of controversies over the nature and causes of structural transformation of Javanese rural society.

Alternative Explanations of Agrarian Change

Most analyses of agrarian change in Java stem from a notion of precapitalist agrarian relations based largely on Geertz's *Agricultural Involution* (1963). The essence of Geertz's argument is that Dutch colonial penetration tended to reinforce a highly symmetrical and egalitarian social structure ("shared poverty"), which enabled the absorption of massive increases in population by the peasant sector ("involution"). Because the ecological conditions of Java allowed major export crops (notably, sugar) to be integrated into the peasant wet-rice economy, the Dutch

---

1. These changes are described and discussed in detail in chap. 7.
2. See Stoler for an analysis of harvesting arrangements; she calls attention to some of the fallacies inherent in the sterotyped view (1977a).

were able to extract an enormous surplus while distorting but not transforming the social organization of rural society.

The predominant view now is that the "Green Revolution" of the late 1960s and 1970s has been primarily responsible for the disintegration of shared poverty and the rapid spread of agrarian capitalism. The dynamic in this process is usually identified as the commercialization of production through the purchase of inputs, which in turn has led to the emergence of capitalist labor relations. The transformation of rural labor relations is thus seen as a profit-maximizing response to technologically determined opportunities. Among those who adhere to the general view that modern rice technology has precipitated the spread of rural capitalism, there are, however, several divergent analyses of the nature of the commercialization process and its long-term consequences; these reflect widely used paradigms of rural development and agrarian change.

First is the neoclassical approach, typified by the arguments of Leiserson et al. discussed above. These authors do not undertake a conceptual analysis of rural change, but it is clear that they interpret "commercialization" primarily in terms of "traditional village institutions and practices" having been replaced by competitive labor market conditions (1978: 34). The notion that wages and employment are determined by the market rather than by "traditional" or "institutional" forces in turn forms the basis of their contention that returns to labor in non-agricultural rural activities more or less approximate those in agriculture and, consequently, that growth in the economy as a whole has prevented the downward pressure on wages that would be expected with the disintegration of poverty sharing.

Although the second approach is commonly regarded as Marxist, it stems more directly from Lenin's analysis of agrarian differentiation in nineteenth-century Russia (1899). According to Lenin, the penetration of capitalism in the countryside leads inexorably to the polarization of landholdings and the development of impersonal wage labor relations; hence the disappearance of the peasantry and the emergence of opposing classes of kulaks and proletarians. Consistent with both Lenin and the neoclassical approach, neo-Leninist explanations of

contemporary agrarian change in Java identify the commercialization of labor relations as the key mechanism of rural
transformation (Mortimer 1975; Gordon 1978). However,
while neoclassical analysts regard rural labor markets as having
been instrumental in facilitating widespread participation in
economic growth, neo-Leninists view the spread of wage labor
relations in terms of intensifying labor exploitation and the ex-
acerbation of social tensions. Mortimer, in particular, argues
that a sharp rift is emerging between a "loyal and powerful kulak class" and the rural poor, and he suggests that this is giving
rise to growing class consciousness and conflict.

The third and most widely accepted interpretation is that the
spread of technology together with population growth has resulted in declining welfare because the large farmers have re-
neged on their customary obligations to provide poor villagers
with income-earning opportunities in order to cut production
costs (Strout 1975; Palmer 1977; Collier et al. 1978). In common with the neo-Leninist approach, those who adhere to this
view (which can broadly be termed neopopulist) maintain that
a process of polarization is underway. The neo-Leninists attrib-
ute the polarization process to forces inherent in the spread of
rural capitalism, but the neopopulists place more direct emphasis on the effects of technology.

The fourth approach to explaining agrarian change in Java
is an adaptation of the neoclassical approach that is aimed at
refuting the neopopulist interpretation. According to this view,
the differentiation process is a consequence not of technologically induced commercialization, but rather of growing population pressure in areas unsuited to modern rice technology.
Proponents of this approach envisage a process whereby

> as the growth of population presses hard on limited land resources
> under constant technology, cultivation frontiers are expanded to
> more marginal land and greater amounts of labor applied per unit
> of cultivated land; the cost of food production increases and food
> prices rise; in the long run, laborers' income will decrease to a sub-
> sistence minimum barely sufficient to maintain stationary popula-
> tion and all the surplus will be captured by landlords as increased
> land rent. (Hayami and Kikuchi 1982: 192)

[margin notes:]
③ neopopulist – mix of Lenin, role of ... labor displacing tech... + slight malthus (role of tech. could be seen from labor-process marxist view)

④ neoclassical + malthus

Conversely, they argue that agricultural technology and infrastructure are effective means for preventing growing poverty and inequality. The rationale seems to be that technology determines factor shares, which in turn determine institutional forms.

The problem with theories that view rural exchange exclusively in terms of technological, market, and demographic forces is that none is able to account for some important features of labor processes in rural Java. The neoclassical approach is least able to explain the micro evidence that shows forms of agricultural labor organization that diverge from the standard competitive model, as well as a diverse structure of nonagricultural rural activities, many of which yield lower returns to labor than agricultural wages.[3] The difficulties encountered by the other three approaches are less stark, but nonetheless apparent. Husken, for instance, demonstrates that, contrary to the neo-Leninist view that the development of impersonal wage labor relations constitutes the primary mechanism of rural capitalist penetration, "traditional labor relations are still being used and adapted by a group of big landowners with strong commercial orientation" (1979: 142). A key feature of these arrangements is that they provide preferential access to some workers, while excluding others. Both the neopopulists and Hayami and Kikuchi recognize that these more complex forms of labor organization are an important part of the differentiation process, but neither is able to explain important parts of the evidence. Contrary to what one would expect on the basis of the neopopulist argument, there does not seem to be any consistent correlation between the extent of adoption of modern rice technology and the emergence or adaptation of institutions tending to limit income-earning opportunities in agriculture. Hayami and Kikuchi, on the other hand, cannot explain the rapidity with which many of these arrangements appeared (or reappeared) in the late 1960s.

---

3. To the extent that these activities occur during slack seasons, they are consistent with the neoclassical model; there is, however, a good deal of evidence showing that these activities often coexist with more remunerative agricultural jobs.

The limited explanatory power of these theories derives from problems in the conceptualization of both labor arrangements and dynamic processes. The Leninist approach is a prime example, because it is the only one of the four that goes beyond a comparative-static view of rural change. Its chief limitation is that it views commercialization as a linear process with uniform consequences. Accordingly, it fails to come to terms with the findings of a growing number of in-depth studies of rural labor arrangements in Java and other countries. These studies frequently show that supposedly "precapitalist" institutions not only survive the development of capitalism in the countryside, but are often reinforced, adapted, and embellished in highly imaginative and varied ways (Bhalla 1976; Bardhan and Rudra 1978, 1980). It is becoming apparent, too, that these institutional arrangements, which often involve labor being tied in with land, credit, and other relations, form the source of the so-called "imperfections" that figure so prominently in the literature on rural labor markets.

One recent branch of the rural labor market literature attempts to explain these more complex institutional arrangements. The model that deals most directly with the problems addressed in this book is one by Bardhan, which explains interlocking contracts in the labor market in terms of employers' efforts to ensure an adequate labor supply in the face of tightening labor market conditions (1979). In Java, however, some of the most important examples of interlocking transactions seem to flourish in slack labor market conditions. Hayami and Kikuchi take account of slackness in the labor market but fail to explain the rapid emergence of these arrangements in the late 1960s (1982).

Generally, the problem with all of these theories is that they omit critically important variables. In particular, the spread of modern rice technology in Java coincided with the transformation of the entire political-economic system, the main element of which was a shift in the state's interests in and relations with the rural sector. Although technological change, commercialization, and population growth are important elements of agrarian change, their effects on rural economy and society have been shaped in important ways by structural forces beyond the rural sector.[4] What is needed, therefore, is a conceptual framework that helps establish the connections between macro political-economic forces and labor processes at the local level.

CONCEPTS AND METHODOLOGY

Concepts

The framework that grows out of the Sukodono study comprises three main levels of analysis:

1. Macro political-economic forces, particularly the state's interests in and relations with different rural groups
2. The structure of relations within rural society, particularly the institutional arrangements to recruit and manage labor
3. The internal organization of the domestic economy, particularly the connection between the position of different gender/age groups and the household's position in the wider economy and society.[5]

The defining feature of my approach is that it rests on a detailed empirical analysis of the organization and deployment of labor at the level of the household, and its purpose is to identify the connections and feedback processes among the different levels. In chapter 8 this framework is used to interpret the significance of the evidence from Sukodono and other villages; to develop hypotheses about the changes that have taken place since the late 1970s; and to identify the agrarian issues that are emerging as oil revenues shrink.

The chief contrast with the Leninist approach lies in the way in which dynamic processes are conceptualized. By viewing causality as circular instead of unidirectional and linear, I can better identify the processes that often give rise to complex patterns of agrarian differentiation.

4. This point was first made by White in the context of a critique of demographic determinism (1976b). Sajogyo calls attention to the importance of changes in the state's position vis-à-vis the rural sector (1974a).

5. The international context is, of course, also important. Chapter 3 contains a discussion of foreign aid and investment in Indonesia in relation to domestic policy.

The other obvious set of contrasts is with the neoclassical paradigm. According to the neoclassical model of the household, variations in access to income opportunities are the direct consequence of differences in internal resource endowments, both human and physical. Given these endowments, everyone faces essentially the same potential set of "choices," defined by the wages and prices generated by the impersonal workings of factor and product markets; the choices that people actually make are governed by their preferences, which are assumed to be exogenously given.

Both the neoclassical theory of the household and econometric estimates of household models rely on the assumption that labor markets are perfectly competitive (e.g., Barnum and Squire 1979), thereby totally evading what is often one of the most interesting and important agrarian problems. The other key element of the neoclassical household model concerns the way in which the preferences of different household members are aggregated within a joint utility function. The method of aggregation assumes that the (male) head of household acts "as if" he were a benevolent dictator who, with Solomonian wisdom and compassion, internalizes the preferences of subordinate members of the household. The hitch, of course, is that these preferences are not always (if ever) identical or even compatible, let alone fixed and unaffected by socioeconomic change (Folbre 1984; Jones, C., 1983).

I shall address both of these problems, the first more comprehensively than the second. Indeed, my prime goal is to identify the economic, social, and political forces that structure and differentiate the options available to different households and, in turn, to understand how the actions of a certain group influences its own access to opportunities as well as that of others.

The third body of literature that bears on my approach concerns the analysis of rural labor markets. A question that has dominated this literature for many years is precisely that which forms the core of the macro data debate outlined above: why do rural labor markets often seem not to clear? This apparent anomaly has given rise to many theories of rural labor market "imperfections" that, in essence, view labor arrangements as deviations from a competitive norm. The two most sophisticated versions are summarized in chapter 7. On the surface at least, the evidence from Sukodono is consistent with two different theories of market imperfections, though on closer examination neither performs very well. More generally, the problems with this approach are that different theories of labor market imperfections can be invoked to explain a given set of evidence and also that totally contradictory sets of evidence can both be attributed to labor market imperfections.

A more recent theme in the rural labor market literature concerns the way in which rural labor relations are often tied in with land and credit—the so-called "interlinkage" literature—that reflects economists' recognition of patronage as an important agrarian phenomenon. This literature constitutes a debate between those who characterize such arrangements as being semi-feudal and operating so as to perpetuate agricultural backwardness and those who maintain that they are based primarily on market principles and are, in effect, consistent with the development of rural capitalism. This debate echoes the central issues discussed earlier in the context of Lenin's theory of agrarian change. The view that interlocking transactions are semi-feudal derives from Lenin's opinion that more diffuse relations between workers and employers constitute obstacles to capitalist development. The contrary position can be seen as an effort to explain how and why supposedly precapitalist forms not only persist, but sometimes expand in the process of capitalist development.

The central elements in this latter approach are laid out by Bardhan in his review of the literature on interlocking factor markets (1980). Drawing a sharp distinction between what he terms "market" relationships and those based primarily on extraeconomic coercion, Bardhan argues that most of the multistranded arrangements to be found in India and other contemporary poor agrarian economies are market relations: "Indebtedness to one's employer for consumption credit or homestead does not necessarily make one a bonded laborer, just as an office worker borrowing from his provident fund account or living in company quarters is not an unfree laborer, even though he may not be in a position to switch jobs easily for *economic* reasons" (1980: 84). The explicit implication is that, because these are market relations, they can be analyzed in abstraction from the political, legal, and ideological context within which they occur.

This assumption forms the basis of a series of microchoice-theoretic models of market interlinkages. These models fall into two main categories. First is a model by Bardhan, who predicts that the importance of tied contracts will increase with economic progress (1979). The rationale is essentially similar to the recruitment model outlined earlier: with a general tightening of the labor market and greater emphasis on the timeliness of operations required by new technology, employers will use labor contracts that provide such side benefits as cheap credit to insure an adequate labor force. A second set of models analyzes interlinkages within sharecropping contracts (Braverman and Srinivasan 1981; Braverman and Stiglitz 1982; Mitra 1982). Although these models vary somewhat in their emphasis, the authors' main theme is that the interlocking of subsidized credit with labor fulfills a supervisory function. In essence, these contracts are seen as an attempt to improve allocative efficiency in the face of moral hazard (Mitra 1982; Braverman and Stiglitz 1982).

My analysis of rural labor arrangements recognizes that the institutional arrangements that emerge as development proceeds are often (although not always) more complex than simple, impersonal wage labor transactions, and focus on labor recruitment and control. However, two important elements distinguish my approach from the interlinkage models: the analysis of contract enforcement, and explicit attention to the exercise of power and social control.[6]

One anomalous feature of the sharecropping models just discussed is that they take recourse to something very close to "extra-economic coercion" in order to explain contract enforcement. In contrast, I shall show how, in many agrarian labor arrangements, the mechanism that ensures effort is the worker's perception of being in a comparatively privileged position; conversely, from the employer's point of view, the essential feature of this strategy of labor management is the selective extension of "privileges" to particular workers. An inevitable

6. These arguments are developed further in Hart (forthcoming).

consequence is, of course, labor market segmentation. Unlike in Bardhan's recruitment model, however, this segmentation can arise in slack labor market conditions as well as in seasonally tight ones. When labor markets are slack, employers often use job security as a mechanism of labor management, the effectiveness of which is contingent on a pool of "underemployed" labor. Many of the institutional arrangements observed in different parts of Java embody precisely these principles.

Rural labor arrangements cannot be understood simply as market phenomena, however. The key to explaining variations and changes in labor arrangements lies in understanding how relations between workers and employers are shaped by larger power structures, which are, in turn, influenced by labor relations. A crucial determinant of strategies of labor recruitment and management is whether and to what extent employers seek to influence workers in spheres not directly related to the labor process. Employers' needs to exercise social control can arise from social and political forces as well as from the labor process itself. The challenge, therefore, is to explain the interface and tension between the recruitment and discipline of labor on the one hand and the exercise of social control on the other. This is central to an analysis of institutional change that comes about partly as a consequence of changing macroeconomic-political conditions and partly as a consequence of the internal tensions and contradictions generated by institutional arrangements. In the case of Java, the political and administrative changes brought about by the New Order regime in the late 1960s were responsible for dramatic shifts in the power of employers relative to workers, and the transformation of agrarian labor arrangements can only be explained in the context of these and subsequent changes in the position of different rural groups in relation to the larger system.

Evidence and Methodology

The detailed evidence on the deployment and organization of labor that forms the core of this book was gathered in 1975–1976 from a sample of eighty-six households.[7] Sukodono, the

7. The selection of the sample and methods of data collection are described in detail in Hart (1978).

site of the study, is located 30 km. west of the city of Semarang on the northern coastal plain, which is one of the main rice- and sugar-producing regions of Java. As with any village, Sukodono is in certain respects a special case. It is comparatively well-endowed in terms of the quality of rice land, and population density is somewhat lower than the norm for lowland rice villages. Extensive sugar production in the region, as well as brackish water fishponds, provide a wider range of economic activity than is often the case in villages located at some distance from an urban center.

In many other ways, however, Sukodono exemplifies some of the key features of Javanese agrarian structure. First, the small average farm size (0.6 ha) masks a highly concentrated pattern of access to and control over productive resources, notably land. In Sukodono less than 10 percent of village households controlled nearly 60 percent of the land and most of the other productive resources, a degree of concentration fairly typical of lowland rice villages. Most members of this landowning elite were connected with village government either directly or through close kinship ties, and were from families that had historically occupied a dominant position in the village. At the other extreme, about 45 percent of the households were either landless or near-landless. Rates of landlessness of this magnitude are also quite common in lowland areas. Many of those with small landholdings had fallen into debt due to pest problems with modern rice varieties in the early 1970s and had entered into complex credit arrangements with large landowners that involved partial loss of their control over their land. In consequence, they were becoming increasingly dependent on wage labor income.

The second important characteristic of the social organization of production in Sukodono, which reflects general patterns, is that most agricultural (and fishpond) labor was hired. Even those operating the most minute plots sometimes hired labor to perform peak season operations, but the bulk of labor hiring was done by the small group of large landowners.

Demand for agricultural labor over the course of the survey rose with the spread of pest-resistant rice technology, primarily as a consequence of shorter growing cycles that allowed more intensive cropping. Access to work was, however, highly differentiated and was mediated in part by the land-debt contracts mentioned above. These arrangements were designed *to keep labor cheap and manageable* by providing job security to a select group of workers, while simultaneously excluding others. Many of those excluded from these more "preferential" arrangements were landless people whose insecure position in the labor market was compounded by their almost total dependence on the market for food grains, which was characterized by wide price fluctuations. The survival of these households was contingent upon the deployment of huge amounts of male, female and child labor to activities yielding very low returns.

Although the institutional forms in Sukodono had been shaped by a specific set of local conditions, they functioned like labor arrangements observed in many other parts of Java and created a division between those incorporated into comparatively secure contractual arrangements and those whose position in the labor market was far more tenuous.

A notable feature of these exclusionary arrangements was their tendency to disappear and reappear, sometimes with astonishing speed. Patterns such as these were recorded during the colonial period, and from the late 1960s on exclusionary labor arrangements reemerged in many areas of Java after a period of decline. The theories of agrarian change that attempt to explain these patterns simply in terms of technology and population growth are, as indicated earlier, unable to account for important parts of the evidence.

In order both to explain the emergence and disappearance of these types of arrangements and to appreciate their more general significance in terms of agrarian differentiation, I shall view them within the explicit context of wider political and economic structures.

Part I
THE NATIONAL CONTEXT

Ultimately . . . the question of Indonesia's direction lies in the great silent sector of society, the peasant mass that floats—or as some would have it, sinks—under the New Order. In the parliamentary period, the Communists organized them; during Guided Democracy Sukarno exhorted them; but it may be that future historians will conclude that it was Suharto who brought them decisive change.

Ruth T. McVey,
"The *Beamtenstaat* in Indonesia"

2

CHANGING RELATIONS BETWEEN
PEASANTS AND THE STATE

The prevalent view of agrarian change in Java is that the introduction of modern rice technology has set in motion a process of commercialization that has stimulated the rapid spread of rural capitalism and attenuated conditions of shared poverty. Many who hold this view thus deny the contemporary relevance of Geertz's notions of agricultural involution and shared poverty but accept his central contention that Dutch colonial rule facilitated extraction from the Javanese peasantry "without changing fundamentally the structure of indigenous society" (1963: 47).

It is this view that my analysis seeks to challenge. A growing body of historiographical research questions the validity of involution and shared poverty, and points instead to a process of disintegration of older structures along with the emergence of new and qualitatively different forms of social organization. In fact, Javanese rural society underwent a significant transformation over the course of the colonial period.

This revisionist view of Javanese rural society during the colonial period informs my analysis of the contemporary character of the Javanese rural elite and their relations with other rural groups and the state. Contradicting the standard approach, I shall argue that the Javanese rural elite is not simply a capitalist class that has emerged in response to technologically induced commercialization. Just as dominant rural groups were coopted during the colonial period, the contemporary rural elite has, since the late 1960s, been transformed into a class of favored clients of the state. The process through which the state has redefined its agrarian interests has shaped the conse-

19

quences of technological change in agriculture and has created conditions for significant changes in social relations within rural society.

POLITICAL CHANGE IN JAVA:
AN HISTORICAL OVERVIEW

The connections between national political and economic forces and agrarian processes are best understood in their historical context. Conventional descriptions of "traditional" Javanese rural society have overstated its egalitarian character, perhaps because there was no landed gentry analogous to the zamindars of the Indian subcontinent. According to the precolonial system of appanage, the king granted his officials (the *priyayi* or nobility) the right to extract produce and labor from groups of peasants (known as *cacah* or service units), but no direct property rights. Not only was the appanage defined in terms of numbers of people rather than territorially, but the following of an appanage holder was often scattered to preclude the consolidation of competing power centers (Moertono 1974; Onghokham 1977; Breman 1980).[1] Within rural society, the pattern of access to land was highly differentiated, however, and a class of dependent landless households existed long before the full-scale colonial exploitation of Java.[2] Moreover, contrary to the stereotypical view of the traditional Javanese village as a closed "little republic" extending from time immemorial, villages only became administrative and territorial units in the early nineteenth century at the instigation of the colonial state (van Niel 1964, 1983).

Over the course of the colonial period, the *priyayi* were absorbed as functionaries into the huge state apparatus con-

---

1. "Intermediaries existed in all sorts of gradations and were, moreover, interlinked in an inferior-superior hierarchy with connotations of patronage. . . . At each progressive link in the chain a part of the collected surplus, levied in produce and labor, was siphoned off" (Breman, 1980: 17).

2. Onghokham (1977) describes how in Madiun (East Java), the lowest stratum of peasant society (the *numpang*) had no heritable land rights and were almost entirely dependent on the *sikep* (nuclear villager) class. *Numpang* peasants who were married and had a long-standing relationship with the *sikep* were sometimes granted rotating shares in the communal (*lanyah*) land of the village. Onghokham argues that the main function of the *lanyah* land was to provide an inducement to laborers to remain in the village because land was relatively abundant and labor scarce in precolonial Java.

structed by the Dutch, and the upper echelons of the colonial civil service in turn formed the core of the national elite in the postindependence era (McVey 1970; Emmerson 1976; Sutherland 1979). The bureaucratic and urban orientation of the dominant class is central to understanding relations between peasants and the state as they changed over time.

The Colonial Period

The Dutch East India Company initiated commerce in the Indonesian archipelago in the late sixteenth century, and by 1798 (when it went bankrupt) its armies had annexed most of Java. The process of extraction from the peasantry was intensified with the introduction of new crops, primarily coffee and indigo, and the Company made extensive use of the indigenous system of intermediaries. Whatever the intentions of the Company, in practice the payments that were made accrued to the Javanese regents and those who "farmed" whole villages for the regents (Wertheim 1964: 240).

With the bankruptcy of the Dutch East India Company, authority shifted directly to the Dutch government. Governor-General Daendels contemplated the introduction of a land tax of one-fifth of the gross produce but finally decided that "'until the Javanese has made further progress toward civilization . . . his work under compulsion must take the place of regular taxes'" (Furnivall 1944: 65). He thus continued the system of forced production of export crops but ordered that cultivators should receive some payment.

During the brief British interregnum (1811–1816) under Sir Thomas Stamford Raffles, the structure of colonial administration underwent major changes. The foundation was laid for the establishment of the village as the primary administrative unit. Whereas the Dutch were mainly interested in the supply of tropical produce, Britain was seeking markets for her growing textile industry. In line with the more liberal approach that this necessitated, Raffles abolished forced labor and introduced a system of land tax (termed "landrent") that bypassed the regents and their intermediaries, and established a direct link between the state and the peasantry. Village headmen were made responsible for subdividing the land and collecting the landrent, which amounted to the cash value of 40 percent of gross produce, and a capitation tax on noncultivators. An enthusiastic adherent of Adam Smith, Raffles judged that "this improved system of political economy . . . by affording that protection to individual industry . . . will ensure to every class of society the equitable and undisturbed enjoyment of the fruits of labour" (Proclamation of 1813, cited by Furnivall 1944: 69). The return of the Dutch in 1816 precluded Javanese peasantry from the enjoyment of British textiles that Raffles intended.

For a while after the reestablishment of Dutch rule, policy tended in the direction defined by Raffles, and the landrent was maintained, although there was a shift from individual to village assessment. By the late 1820s, however, liberal policy was rapidly falling apart. The Dutch treasury was under severe pressure, and the state turned to the more directly extractive methods of earlier times to alleviate its fiscal problems.

One of the most massive instances of forced labor mobilization in recorded history, the "Cultivation System" instituted in 1830 was a huge financial success from the viewpoint of the Dutch government. Described by Governor-General Baud as "the lifebelt on which the Netherlands kept afloat," Java proved to be the most profitable colony in the world.

The basis of the Cultivation System was that, in return for remission of land rents, Javanese peasants had to cultivate government-owned cash crops on one-fifth of village lands, or work sixty-six days a year on government estates or other projects. The system was presented as less onerous than the 40 percent landrent. In practice, however, the burden on the peasantry was immense. Not only was there a considerable degree of official latitude in the degree of extraction, but the system was wide open to abuse by Dutch administrators, as well as by the Javanese regents and their henchmen. The condition that only a fifth of village lands could be used for government cultivation was seldom adhered to, and the extent of corvée labor frequently exceeded the sixty-six days by a considerable margin (van der Kolff 1929).

The official termination of the Cultivation System with the passage of the Agrarian Land Law in 1870 reflected a response to conditions that had, in part, been brought about by the Cultivation System. By the 1860s the Dutch economy was moving rapidly toward industrialization, fueled by the revenues from colonial exploitation and generating growing demand for produce and raw materials. The huge expansion of infrastructure made private enterprise in Java progressively more feasible and attractive, and this was further enhanced by major technological advances in sugar milling. These forces gave rise to considerable pressures from the more "liberal" elements of the Dutch body politic for opening up the colonies to private enterprise and instituting a tenurial system that would allow for the lease and purchase of land from the indigenous population. The "conservative" opposition feared that the dispossession of the peasantry would lead inevitably to a disruption of law and order, and argued strenuously that the existing system should not be forced into a Western mold to which it was unsuited.

The Agrarian Land Law represented a compromise between liberals and conservatives. It enabled private concerns to lease—but not to purchase—native land. The law also "guaranteed the natives possession of their customary rights over land, and made it possible for them to obtain rights of private ownership over land" (Furnivall 1944: 178). In many areas, the Agrarian Land Law substituted forced cultivation of export crops with compulsory leasing of peasants' land for sugar cultivation under what Geertz terms the Corporate Plantation System (1963).

By the late nineteenth century, Dutch interests in the Netherlands Indies were focusing increasingly on the market potential of Javanese rural society: "In [the Dutch] parliament this manufacturing interest grew so strong that in 1896 it could defeat a proposal for import duties, and in 1900 the Chambers of Commerce were showing their sympathy for the Javan in complaints that he had less to spend on clothes" (Furnivall 1944: 227). The Declining Welfare Survey (1904–1905) found that the average Javanese was indeed miserably poor, a condition attributed primarily to population growth.

The outcome of this concern was the so-called "Ethical Policy," whose main objective was to stimulate "native welfare" while maintaining the existing social order insofar as possible. Commercialization proceeded rapidly, however. Over the course of the following decades, a wide range of measures contributed directly and indirectly to growing rural monetization. Taxation was increasingly shifted away from levies on produce and labor to a capitation tax paid in cash, and cottage industry gave way to imported goods, particularly cotton textiles. Deliberate efforts were also made to stimulate peasant agriculture, and comparatively large amounts were allocated to agricultural credit, irrigation, and emigration. By the 1920s, the cultivation of commercial crops by the peasantry had increased markedly; the value of peasant agricultural exports rose from f. 5 million in 1898 to f. 104 million in 1929. Peasant produce as a percentage of total exports increased from 5 to 18 percent but decreased sharply in absolute terms after 1930 when Java was particularly hard hit by the Great Depression (Furnivall 1944: 320).

In 1942 Japan invaded what was to become Indonesia, and the occupation lasted until 1945. Nationalist sentiment gathered force over this period, and in August 1945 Indonesian independence was declared shortly before the Japanese withdrawal. The first four years of the Republic of Indonesia were marked by a protracted war of liberation against the Dutch who returned to reclaim their colonial position in 1945 and did not withdraw until late 1949.

During the Japanese occupation, the peasantry as a whole was subjected to immense pressure. For a brief period during the liberation war, however, it seems that there was a strengthening in the relative position of the peasantry and of some of the weaker groups within it. Three factors were particularly important. First, land taxes were not adjusted to high inflation rates and were rendered negligible. Second, not only was a great deal of peasant indebtedness wiped out by inflation, but, in many instances, Republican officials refused to enforce debt collection. Finally, estate laborers and peasants from adjacent areas took over many of the estate lands for the cultivation of subsistence crops (Kahin 1952: 474–75).

In spite of such levelling tendencies, the view that the dominant tendency was one of intensified "poverty-sharing" and ossification of agrarian structures is highly questionable. Instead,

the weight of evidence points to profound changes in the organization of rural society over the course of the colonial period.

The Sukarno Era and the Rise of the PKI

The central feature of the Sukarno era (1949–1965) was the
rise of the Indonesian Communist party (the Partai Komunis
Indonesia or PKI). Conflicts of interest between urban and rural areas and within rural society were the motive force behind
the gathering strength of the PKI and were in turn intensified
by it. Indeed, the present structure of Indonesian society has
been shaped in important ways by the violent reactions to the
PKI's strategy of mass agrarian mobilization.

In the early postindependence period (1949–1953), parliament was dominated by conservative factions in the Nationalist
(PNI or Partai Nasional Indonesia) and Masyumi parties. Re-
acting to the chaos of the revolution and the destruction it had
wrought, the early cabinets were intensely concerned with re-
construction and growth of the economy, strengthening law
and order, and regularizing the bureaucracy (Feith 1962).

The priorities attached to production, fiscal stability, and administrative rationalization lost ground rapidly after 1953
along with growing pressures from the exrevolutionary group
for a larger share of political and economic power (Feith 1962),
and the period between 1953 and 1956 was one of "serious
partisan conflict, extensive party penetration of the villages,
and the declining legitimacy of parliamentary government"
(Liddle 1978: 174).

After the 1955 elections, attention at the national level came
increasingly to be focused on external issues, and most of the
parties tended "to place decreasing emphasis on cultivating
their mass following and more on maneuver in the insular
world of Djakarta politics" (McVey 1969: 22). The sole exception to this general retrenchment of agrarian political mobilization was an intensified PKI effort to elicit rural support.

In the early postindependence period, the PKI adopted a
gradualist approach to peasant mobilization, stressing village

welfare activities and in many villages depending quite heavily on the support of relatively wealthy peasants. Until about 1958, the penetration that the PKI was able to achieve was determined primarily by the strength of prior loyalties to the PNI and Islamic parties. There were two main patterns of PKI support: In multiparty villages, PKI support tended to come from unaccommodated youth and other radicalized elements; in single party villages, by contrast, the leading Communists were often those who had the most prestige and could command the greatest patronage in traditional terms: "men of substance, either in land or in political authority, and frequently in both" (Mortimer 1974: 278). Such leaders were quite capable of promoting the kinds of welfare programs that were the chief plank of the PKI's strategy in the early and mid-1950s. Generally, "while the PNI approached the peasant through the traditional channels of the aristocratic and bureaucratic *prijaji* elite, the PKI appealed directly to his interests" (Lev 1966: 9).

The growing penetration of the state apparatus by political parties was another factor that differentiated the PKI from the other parties. Anderson identifies two particularly important elements in this process (1983). First, the parties relied heavily on access to the state in order to generate resources. This meant that they were in a position to grant licenses, contracts, and other benefits in order to forge mutually beneficial relationships with the wealthy Chinese community. Second, enrolling their supporters within the state apparatus was a cheap and easy way of rewarding them. The PKI relied less on these tactics and focused instead on expanding and consolidating its agrarian base. The payoffs were clearly evident in the 1957 regional elections when the PKI emerged as the largest party in Java.

The electoral success of the PKI was in part responsible for the abandonment of the parliamentary system and the institution in 1958 of "Guided Democracy." Another major element in the demise of parliamentary democracy was the growing political and economic strength of the army to which Sukarno had given control over nationalized Dutch estates in 1957. At the same time, the other parties "participated enthusiastically in their own emasculation," mostly because of their fears of being overwhelmed by the PKI (Lev 1966).

Guided Democracy can thus be seen as an effort by Sukarno to preserve and protect the national elite from its inadequate rooting in the larger society (McVey 1969). In the process, he became increasingly dependent on the PKI and the mass support that it represented in order to maintain its bargaining position vis-à-vis the army. Simultaneously, the PKI's fear of the army left it with few options other than to ally itself with Sukarno (Feith 1963).

In 1959 the PKI launched a campaign aimed at more systematic peasant mobilization than before, although its demands were still fairly moderate (Mortimer 1974: 276). This strategy was partly a response to the restrictions that the army had placed on the urban activities of the PKI. Because the party depended on Sukarno's protection and its appeal to Sukarno lay in the size of its organizational base, an expanded and more systematic approach to peasant mobilization appeared the safest and most productive strategy. Mortimer suggests that the PKI's turn to the peasantry was also an effort to placate its radical wing, which chafed at the constraints imposed by Guided Democracy.

The initial demands of the PKI actually fell far short of the land reform legislation passed in 1960. The PKI proposed that sharecroppers receive a minimum share of 60 percent and that land redistribution be confined to holdings of foreigners and those who had participated in antigovernment rebellions. The initiative for land reform came from Sukarno, but the PKI subsequently advocated a policy of "land to the tiller," which would have abolished absentee ownership and all forms of sharecropping and renting. This move was violently opposed by Moslem groups who argued that *adat* law prohibited the alienation of proprietary land rights. A compromise supported by Sukarno and the Minister of Agriculture accepted the radical position in principle but argued that it should be accomplished in stages, the first of which was the determination of minimum and maximum landholdings.

The PKI accepted the compromise, together with a set of

restrictions on sharecropping. In September 1960, the Basic Agrarian Law (*Undang-Undang Pokok Agraria*) and the associated Sharecropping Act (*Undang-Undang Pokok Bagi Hasil*) were passed, replacing the dualistic system of property rights embodied in the 1870 legislation. Maximum landholdings were defined according to population densities and land types. The provisions were absurdly generous by Javanese standards—the law stated that the government would endeavor to provide every peasant household with a minimum of two hectares of arable land (a goal impossible to achieve in Java, given population densities)—but they contained a number of loopholes. Priority in implementation was given to articles 7, 10, and 17 of the Basic Agrarian Law, which forbade ownership of more than the permitted maximum of land, forbade absentee ownership, and gave the government authority to redistribute surplus land.

Not unexpectedly, the expropriation of surplus land proceeded slowly. In 1961 a hierarchical system of land reform committees had been set up, which at the village level were under the "guidance" of the village administration (Utrecht 1969). The resistance of the large landowners to land redistribution was supported by the Moslem parties and by powerful groups within the PNI; opposition was hardened by the failure of the state to pay compensation. In a sharp break with previous policies, the PKI in 1963 embarked on a strategy of class-based mobilization in the form of the *aksi sepihak* (unilateral actions) campaign, which involved the peasant wing of the PKI (the Barisan Tani Indonesia) in a series of land takeovers. The *aksi* campaign was conceived by the party as a means of shifting the balance of power in rural society and mobilizing peasant support for "a more peaceful variant of Mao Tse-tung's strategy of surrounding the cities from the countryside—the object of which was to force the Indonesian elite to disgorge at least a measurable amount of its national power to the PKI" (Mortimer 1975: 4).

The PKI campaign took place in the context of intensified conflict between the PKI and the army, the erosion of Sukarno's ability to play different groups off against one another, and extreme economic instability in the form of burgeoning inflation.

The conflict culminated in the abortive coup of 1965, the massive slaughter of PKI supporters, and the takeover of power by the New Order regime in 1966.

The New Order

The threat posed by the PKI served to unite a number of diverse groups in the period immediately after the coup. The coalition that initially supported General Suharto comprised most of the senior army officers, the devout Islamic community (an urban entrepreneurial group and rural landowning and religious elites), and a middle class of senior bureaucrats, professionals, and intellectuals. Subsequently, there has been a steady concentration of political and economic power in the military, in conjunction with an erosion of the support of many of the nonmilitary members of the coalition. Initially, however, a close symbiotic relationship existed between the army and the other groups. The latter provided the army with legitimation and substantial economic, political, and social concessions; in return the army promised economic stabilization and rationalization, restoration of the rule of law, and an end to Sukarno's foreign policy, which was seen by many as disruptive and destructive (Weinstein 1976).

In addition, the military offered the urban-oriented elite protection from its inadequate rooting in the larger society by suppressing any real challenge from below (McVey 1969). Hence, one key dimension of the New Order state's interests in the rural sector was insuring agrarian "law and order" and preventing the resurgence of agrarian mobilization, which could be used to challenge power at the center. Maintaining tight control over the rural sector has remained a constant theme of New Order policy, even though the instruments of control have become more diverse.

The second main focus of the New Order's agrarian strategy has been on increasing rice production and procurement. Rice policies have undergone some important changes under the New Order and have also tended to move in an opposite direction from policies toward other sectors. In the initial years of the New Order, macroeconomic policy was marked by a general tendency toward trade liberalization and domestic decontrol, but rice policies were interventionist and coercive. Since the early 1970s bureaucratic controls in most sectors of the economy have proliferated, but rice policies have shown a trend toward emphasizing and supporting individual incentives.

Some important insights into the forces that underlie the puzzling and seemingly contradictory aspects of policy under the New Order have recently been provided by Anderson who contends that the policy outcomes of the New Order are best understood as expressions of state interests: "the consistent *leitmotiv* of the New Order governance has been the strengthening of the state-qua-state" (1983: 488).

Developing these arguments requires looking more closely at the key political-administrative changes brought about by the New Order. To appreciate the profound political importance of these changes, one needs to view the bureaucracy in historical perspective (Sutherland 1979; Anderson 1983). The size and dominance of the state apparatus has long been a distinctive feature of Indonesia. During the colonial period, there were nine times as many European administrators relative to the indigenous population as in British India, yet they constituted only about 10 percent of the entire apparatus: "This situation, in turn, was the last stage of a long process in which various strata of (largely Javanese) native ruling classes had, since the mid-nineteenth century, been absorbed, assimilated and encapsulated into an ever more centralized, disciplined and streamlined colonial Beamtenstaat" (Anderson 1983: 480). The state machinery was virtually destroyed during the Japanese war occupation, and Sukarno never succeeded in restoring its dominance and effectiveness. Instead, the bureaucracy increasingly became the arena of political conflict. Penetration of the state apparatus was one of the chief methods that political parties used in order to expand in the 1950s and, as mentioned earlier, during the period of Guided Democracy Sukarno resorted to bureaucratic inflation as a means of coping with interparty conflict. By the end of the Sukarno period, the bureaucracy was in a state of complete chaos. Not only had it increased enormously in size (between 1940 and 1968 the number of civil servants rose from 250,000 to 2,500,000), but it was also largely out of control. The army, by contrast, had considerably strengthened its position.

Administrative reform under the New Order has taken the form of political purging, together with militarizing and streamlining the bureaucracy and ensuring the discipline and allegiance of civil servants. Measures ostensibly designed to ensure bureaucratic loyalty serve in practice to ensure the dominance of Golkar, the electoral machine of the government.[3] The principle of "monoloyalty" is enforced by Korpri, an organizational arm of Golkar to which all civil servants are required to belong. Accordingly, as Emmerson observes, the prohibition on civil servants' engaging in political activity amounts in effect to a ban on non-Golkar activity (1978). Other parties are permitted a nominal existence, but they are tightly controlled by this and other methods.

The class base of Golkar and the New Order thus consists primarily of the *priyayi* bureaucratic elite and is, as Anderson observes, similar to that of the old Nationalist party, the PNI:

> [The] key difference is that Golkar articulates the interests of the state-qua-state, and the PNI merely the interests of the class from which many functionaries of the state have been drawn. In effect, that class has been told that its interests will be served *only* through the mediation of the *apparat*. (1983: 492)

Another distinctive feature of the New Order is the way in which the bureaucracy has been militarized. At the cabinet level, military officers have been replaced by civilians with academic degrees, but the percentage of military officers in important subcabinet positions has risen sharply (Emmerson 1978: 100–105). At lower levels of the administration, particularly in rural areas, the form of militarization is somewhat different:

> Except for patently insecure areas, the office of subdistrict head (*camat*) generally has been left to civilians. Instead of risking its overextension by replacing these with its own men, the army in 1974 began to give military training to some of the better educated *camats*. . . . Future graduates of this program would receive officer

3. Golkar is an acronym for *Golongan Karya* (functional groups). For a discussion of how Golkar is organized and used by the New Order, see Emmerson (1976) and Anderson (1983).

status in the army reserve. The goal of this kind of socialization is apparently to strengthen local administration against any future emergency and to make the *camats* . . . more loyal and responsive to their military superiors in civilian government. (Emmerson 1978: 103)

In its efforts to maintain control over the rural sector, the New Order has also undertaken a massive restructuring of political and administrative institutions at the village level. These policies have been designed explicitly to preclude the resurgence of agrarian mobilization and to contain any threat of the type posed by the PKI during the Sukarno era.

The massive changes in the nature of the state and its position vis-à-vis the rural sector form the essential background for the analysis of the structural transformation of rural society. They are also central to understanding the contemporary character of the rural elite. In order to develop more fully the argument that the rural elite are clients of the New Order state rather than simply a capitalist class that has emerged in response to technologically determined commercialization, I shall return to historical debate and trace some of the chief ways in which macro political-economic forces have both influenced and been shaped by agrarian processes.

THE STATE AND AGRARIAN PROCESSES

The Colonial Period

The central issue in the debate over the agrarian structure in Java is whether, as Geertz argues, colonial rule served to ossify and rigidify "traditional" rural society or whether it was associated with the emergence of a fundamentally different system of social relations.

Geertz's contention that colonial rule in Java reinforced a highly egalitarian agrarian structure rests primarily on the ecological characteristics of wet-rice (*sawah*) cultivation. According to Geertz, the enormous surplus that the Dutch were able to extract from the imposition of sugar cultivation was only partially attributable to Javanese peasants' producing their own food while also working as sugar laborers; this system of cheap labor could perpetuate itself because of the almost infinite capacity of wet-rice cultivation to absorb additional labor while maintaining a more or less constant marginal product. The ecological symbiosis between wet-rice and sugar cultivation was in turn linked with rising population densities, and all three operated to reinforce one another: "The more numerous and better irrigated the [rice] terraces are the more sugar can be grown; and the more people a seasonal, readily available, resident labor force (a sort of part-time proletariat) supported by these terraces during the nonsugar portion of the cycle, can grow sugar" (Geertz 1963: 56).

"Shared poverty" refers to the set of institutional arrangements through which the involutionary process was achieved:

> Under pressure of increasing numbers and limited resources Javanese village society did not bifurcate, as did that of so many other underdeveloped nations, into a group of large landlords and a group of oppressed near-serfs. Rather it maintained a comparatively high degree of social and economic homogeneity by dividing the economic pie into a steadily increasing number of minute pieces, a process to which I have referred elsewhere as "shared poverty." (Geertz 1963: 97)

Although Geertz argued initially that poverty sharing was achieved through a "near-equal fractionalization of landholdings" (1956: 141), his later work places far greater emphasis on work and income-sharing arrangements. In particular, he identifies sharecropping as one of the key mechanisms whereby the homogeneity of Javanese rural society was maintained (1963: 99–100).

The major shifts in policy that took place over the course of the colonial period—in particular the abandonment of forced labor under the Cultivation System (1830–1870) and the passage of the Agrarian Land Law of 1870, which heralded the opening up of sugar cultivation to private enterprise—did not, in Geertz's view, make much difference at the village level: "Sugar . . . continued its mutualistic relationship with wet rice in but slightly changed guise" (1963: 86), and shared poverty was in consequence intensified. By the 1950s, Geertz claims, the process that first emerged in the sugar regions had spread all over Java: he refers to population figures showing "an assimilation of more and more of the island to the demographic and, one presumes, the social conditions prevailing in the densest ones in the earlier period" (1963: 126).

Early critiques by authors who called into question the historical accuracy of Geertz's analysis (Lyon 1970; White 1974, 1976b; Stoler, 1977a) are increasingly being confirmed by a growing body of historiographical researchers (Alexander and Alexander 1978, 1979, 1982; Elson 1978; Husken 1981; Kano 1980; Knight 1982; Kumar 1980; Onghokham 1977; van Niel 1983).[4] A consistent finding of several of these authors is that the "ecological symbiosis" between rice and sugar, which forms the core of the involution thesis, is highly doubtful. In the first place, the ecological requirements of sugar are not identical with those of wet rice (Sajogyo 1976; Alexander and Alexander 1978); instead, it seems that, during the nineteenth century, the Dutch deliberately adapted sugarcane technology to irrigated areas in order to take advantage of the abundant labor in those regions (Sajogyo 1976). Moreover, because irrigation systems for maximizing sugar production are quite different from those for maximizing rice production, the insertion of sugar into a rice-growing regime entails considerable disruption (Alexander and Alexander 1978).

When broken down by region, the statistical evidence that Geertz uses to support his claim that sugar, rice, and population growth reinforced one another exhibits correlation among these variables only in areas where the Cultivation System was not practiced (Husken 1981).[5] Consistent with this statistical analysis, several detailed studies of districts along the north coast where sugar cultivation was most heavily enforced during the Cultivation System show that "the diversion of peasant labour to sugarcane production seems to have resulted not in labour-intensification on the *sawah* wet rice fields remaining in paddy cultivation, but in a decline both in labour-intensity and paddy yields, at least during Geertz' 'decisive' period of the mid-19th century" (White 1983: 13).

4. See White for a comprehensive review and analysis of these studies (1983). Additional references cited by White and van Niel (1983) include Carey (1981), Fasseur (1981), and Fernando (1982).

5. Husken concludes that "The only region where high density, high *sawah*ization and high productivity go together is in . . . the heartland of a region where the cultivation system . . . was never introduced" (1981: 20).

If the involution thesis fails to hold up under closer examination, what then of shared poverty? Once again, a picture very different from that painted by Geertz is starting to emerge from the historical evidence. First is the nature of "traditional" rural society. Geertz does not examine precolonial agrarian structure explicitly, merely suggesting by implication that the "traditional" Javanese village was a comparatively homogeneous, tightly knit entity. However, the complex linking of the agrarian base with the center in the late precolonial period involved the segmentation of the rural population into vertical, nonterritorially determined blocks of patrons and their clients, and within the peasantry there was further differentiation based on control over land (Breman 1980; Onghokham 1977).

Available evidence suggests that intensified extraction from the peasantry did not have a uniform levelling effect. Instead, it appears in many instances to have enhanced the position of strategically placed groups and enabled them to extend and reinforce their access to land and the labor of the less privileged. With the shift from the precolonial system of extraction based on the *cacah* (service unit) to the landrent (village-based) system in the early nineteenth century,

> the heads of service units [who] had been the controllers of land and landed arrangements now continued in this function under the new arrangement in which the village was seen as an administrative and territorial unit. Gradually, during the nineteenth century their power position was enhanced, as government regulations became more strictly enforced. They found that they could use their controlling position over land in new ways. Generally speaking, they continued to parcel out the lands to various lower social levels, while they themselves benefitted from their right to special considerations in special headman lands (which were worked for them) and in the right to retain a percentage of the landrent collection. They, along with the entire village administrative hierarchy, were also excused from obligatory labor service [corvée] which had been put back into place again before 1820. (van Niel 1983: 27)[6]

---

6. An important point to which van Neil calls attention is that the Cultivation System was not a uniformly applied policy, but rather a series of local "accommodations" with village headmen.

As the colonial state sought to demarcate the village as a territorially defined, self-governing "little republic" in order to facilitate extraction from it, the position of the village headman was formalized and he became increasingly vulnerable to the dictates of higher authority, subject to censure, incarceration, and dismissal. At the same time, cooperative village heads were often able to profit handsomely from their position. With the shift to the Corporate Plantation System following passage of the Agrarian Land Law in 1870, village heads played a key role in facilitating the sugar companies' access to land and labor: "village heads were insidiously wooed by European and Chinese entrepreneurs, and found themselves receiving suitable 'presents' when satisfactory agreements were concluded with their villages" (Kumar 1980: 586–87).[7]

Detailed studies from north coast areas where the Cultivation System and, subsequently, the Corporate Plantation System were most actively implemented reveal a clear tendency for "village well-to-do's to accumulate land shares and a disproportionate share of the wealth which sugar cultivation brought into the village" (Elson 1978: 28), together with rapidly growing landlessness.[8] At the same time, this process was accompanied by a proliferation of "precapitalist" institutional arrangements—communalization of land tenure, pawning, sharecropping, and so forth—through which land rights were reallocated and the small-landholding peasantry perpetuated. However, such "work-spreading" was not so much a normatively defined effort to provide each villager with a "subsistence niche" as a

7. There is abundant evidence of the ways in which village government officials were able to take advantage of the arbitrary powers bestowed on them in the organization of sugar cultivation. See, e.g., Elson (1978); Knight (1982); and Onghokham (1977).

8. Some evidence that land concentration increased over the course of the colonial period is pointed out by Geertz himself: the mean and modal landholding size observed by Raffles in 1817 was virtually identical to that in the late 1930s, slightly under one hectare (1963: 97). Although some additional land was brought under cultivation, the population increase over the nineteenth century was such that the maintenance of average landholding size must have been accomplished by massive increases in landlessness. Extrapolating from the data on land distribution collected by the Declining Welfare Enquiry, White and Wiradi estimate that by 1904–1905 approximately 55 percent of the total Javanese population owned no land at all (1979: 15). However, the processes that gave rise to increased landlessness could have differed significantly among and within regions.

way to reduce the disproportionate labor obligations that fell on most small landholders.

By the early twentieth century strategically placed rural groups in some areas were actively engaged in accumulation, both within and outside agriculture (Elson 1978; Husken 1979). During the same period, many reports by colonial administrators call attention to the chronic indebtedness, growing landlessness, and immiseration in the lower echelons of village society (White 1983). The ways in which these processes were connected with one another is still not clear, but it is becoming increasingly evident that Javanese rural society was radically transformed over the course of the colonial period, and that the dominant trend was one of profound social and economic differentiation.

As noted earlier, in some areas the processes of differentiation were arrested and perhaps even reversed by the depression, the Japanese war occupation, and the struggle for independence (Kahin 1952). By the 1950s, however, rural differentiation was again clearly evident in many different parts of Java (Jaspan 1961; Jay 1969; Koentjaraningrat 1967; Lyon 1970; Slamet 1968; ten Dam 1961). Indeed, in *The Social History of an Indonesian Town,* Geertz himself calls attention to "something of a large landholders' class, made up of village chiefs and other well-to-do peasants" (1964: 40).

The PKI and Peasant Mobilization

One of the ironies of *Agricultural Involution* is that it

> appeared precisely at the moment when large-scale agrarian conflicts of a pronounced class character were reaching their height, culminating only two years later in the violent crushing of militant small-peasant and landless-worker organizations by the army and Muslim youth groups associated with the landowning classes, who joined in the massacre of hundreds of thousands of men and women. (White 1983: 4)

The rise of the PKI was not just a reflection of agrarian differentiation. Nor was the PKI simply a class-based organization: its rapid expansion was partly due to its incorporation of large landowners. At the same time, the rise of the PKI both reflected and intensified the antagonisms and conflicts that derived from differential access to and control over the means of production.

However, the PKI's ultimate failure, rather than its initial successes, reveals most clearly the distinctive features of Javanese agrarian structure and is also central to understanding the changes which have taken place over the course of the New Order. Although the discussion that follows is in part hypothetical because local-level evidence is sorely lacking for the Sukarno period, it does offer a consistent explanation for the failure of the PKI, cast in terms of the interplay between macropolitical-economic forces and the structure of agrarian relations.

According to Mortimer (one of the most prominent analysts of the PKI), the PKI's strategy of agrarian mobilization was fatally undermined by the strength of traditional cultural-religious attachments:

> The conflict certainly confirmed the strength of vertical attachments to the party- and religious-based organizations among the rural population. The Communists had tried to fight on class lines for once, and to an extent they had succeeded; but in the end, *aliran* loyalties tended to swamp them. The traditional sociocultural cleavages among the population, which had been an important factor in dictating the PKI's strategic avoidance of class agitation in past years, could not be overcome in the short period in which they cultivated a class approach in the villages. (1974: 327)

This explanation derives from Geertz's *aliran* thesis, according to which the cultural-religious values that the parties represented provided a basis for a variety of village-level organizations and formed the primary bond linking the village to the national political and social system (1960). Geertz's stress on ideological schisms meshes neatly with his theory of shared poverty, which also minimizes the importance of horizontal divisions.

The political alignments that emerged in the postindependence period are often viewed in terms of the traditional cultural-religious cleavages in Javanese society. This *aliran* thesis visualizes Javanese society as being split into ideological streams (*alirans*), embodying deeply held sociocultural and religious values that found expression in the postindependence political party system. According to Geertz, the Nationalist party (Partai Nasional Indonesia or PNI) was composed of *priyayi* adherents to the Hindu elements in Javanese syncretism, whereas the *abangan* (commoners) followers of the animistic elements of syncretism tended to be associated with the PKI. Opposing these "nominal" Muslims were the more devout *santri*, the more orthodox of whom were aligned with the Nahdatul Ulama (NU), and the modernists with the Masyumi party.

The evidence that seems to support Mortimer's argument is that the most pronounced levels of agrarian conflict were in the areas of East Java where there were a number of relatively large Muslim (*santri*) landowners, while most of the poor peasants from whom the PKI drew support were *abangan*. One of the devices used by landowners was to cede land to Islamic schools and other religious institutions, thereby using religious appeals both to counter PKI takeovers and to fan anticommunist sentiment (Castles 1966). There are other phenomena that Mortimer's interpretation cannot explain, however, most notably the active participation by poor peasants in the massacres of 1965 and 1966 in certain areas (Wertheim 1968; Utrecht 1969).

An important missing element in Mortimer's analysis is the rapidly deteriorating macroeconomic situation. From a base of 100 in 1954, the consumer price index rose to over 600 in 1961 and reached 61,000 by 1965 (Arndt 1971: 373). Escalating rice prices and a growing gap between government-controlled rice prices and those prevailing in the market resulted in declining state procurement of rice in both relative and absolute terms (Pelzer 1971: 143).

A common view at the time was that, by turning in on itself, the "self-sufficient" rural sector was better able to withstand the effects of inflation. A far more plausible interpretation is that the impact of inflation within the rural sector was highly regressive (Mackie 1971) and that the surplus rice producers found themselves in an increasingly powerful position relative to the landless and poor peasants who depended on the market to meet their food needs. At the same time, growing rural distress placed increasing pressure on the PKI and its peasant wing, the BTI: "The peasantry became more restive, and consequently if the BTI [Barisan Tani Indonesia, the peasant wing of the PKI] and PKI wanted to retain their following they had to take the lead in this rural unrest" (Wertheim 1969: 13).

Although direct evidence is severely limited, one can speculate on ways in which the rural elite could in principal have used their control over rice and other food in order to cope with peasant unrest and possibly also to undermine the PKI's strategy. First, the "open" harvests, which seem to have been quite extensive during this period, can be seen not so much as a normatively defined manifestation of the "poverty-sharing" ethic as a defensive effort on the part of landowners to maintain social stability. Second, the circumstances in which the rural elite found themselves generated both the incentives and the means for extending and reinforcing relations of dependency with poorer groups:

> Most of the richer farmers who still exerted traditional and economic influences on their labourers, were naturally anti-communistic. But so were many of the landless peasants who, however desperate their position might become, would never join the BTI. They remained "loyal to the landowner," or rather "loyal to the party," the party they shared with their landlord. (Utrecht 1969: 83)

It is possible, therefore, that part of the reason why class-based actions failed was that poor peasants were reluctant to jeopardize the security that patronage relations provided; these vertical ties could also help explain the participation by poor peasants in the agrarian massacres that ushered in the New Order regime.

The Rural Elite Under the New Order

The structure of the New Order regime and its stance toward the rural sector in its early phases (1966–1971) was first and foremost a reaction to the threat posed by the PKI. In addition to maintaining control over the rural sector, the New Order regime sought to ensure rice production and procurement. These concerns have endured, but the policies through which they have been pursued have undergone some important changes over the course of the New Order. These elements of continuity and change in the state's agrarian interests and actions are central to understanding the processes of change within the rural sector.

A key issue is the nature of the rural elite and their position in relation to the larger system. Although remarkably little attention has been devoted to this question, two diametrically opposed views have recently been advanced. One is that

> the landlord classes were the most important allies of the military in the 1965–66 period when the New Order was establishing itself. A powerful rural landlord/kulak class constitutes a significant and strategic base of support for the New Order state. In the fifteen years since the coup, the New Order has provided the basis for consolidation and development of a rural landlord/kulak class through provision of rural credit and infrastructure in conjunction with programs introducing high yielding rice varieties, insecticides and fertilizers into agricultural production. (Robison 1982: 58)

The contrary view is that "the agricultural policies of the Suharto government have not been to produce a kulak class or distinctive stratum of 'dominant peasants.' Its rhetoric and ideology point in quite the opposite direction" (Mackie 1983: 27).

The chief problem with Robison's interpretation is that it does not explain the powerful antagonism between rural producers and the state, which suffused agricultural policy in the early years of the New Order. Although an extractive policy toward the rural sector need not necessarily entail alienating dominant rural groups, there are no indications that the state made any concessions to the large producers during the early period. It is equally difficult to support Mackie's interpretation, however. Accumulation by the rural elite over the course of the New Order may in part have been an unintended consequence of policy, but the shifts in policy that have taken place since the early 1970s have entailed a systematic channelling of resources to the powerful rural groups. These and other actions are difficult to reconcile with the notion that the New Order has been primarily concerned with undermining the rural elite.

Many features of rural policy become far clearer when seen

as part of a process through which the state has attempted to coopt and incorporate the rural elite into the state apparatus. This process has involved extending concessions to dominant rural groups, while also tightening control over them. Accordingly, even though the rural elite have been the recipients of considerable benefits, they do not constitute a base of support for the New Order in the conventional sense of being in a position to influence the policy process. By the same token, although there are numerous instances of the state's acting in ways that reveal and reinforce the subordinate position of the rural elite in the political-economic system, the relationship of this group to the state is not unambiguously antagonistic.

This interpretation of the peculiar class character of the Javanese rural elite is closely consistent with Anderson's analysis of the class basis of the New Order State (1983). Anderson does not examine agrarian issues, but his characterization of the New Order, taken in conjunction with the foregoing discussion of dominant rural groups during the colonial and Sukarno periods, sheds light on the contemporary position of the Javanese rural elite.

Some important supporting evidence for the arguments just outlined comes from a closer examination of the 1971 elections, which constituted an important turning point in the New Order's stance vis-à-vis the rural sector. Before 1971, the New Order was actively engaged in establishing hegemony over the rural sector by military and political means. This process entailed extensive penetration of the civilian bureaucracy by the military at all levels, together with the "Golkarization" of the villages and the emasculation of the remaining political parties. The two were often closely connected, because Golkar sub-branches were built around local administrative, police, and military offices (Ward 1974: 189). Golkar's strategy was to recruit patrons who would in turn procure the support of their clientele: "Thus *kijais* [religious leaders] were dislodged from their links with Muslim parties where possible to win over devout Muslims, village officials were obliged to join Golkar so that the population under their influence could more easily be recruited, teachers, individuals of personal authority and so on were sought as procurers of a wider range of supporters for

Golkar" (ibid.: 172). Golkar's military connections also placed it in a position to take advantage of the vulnerability of those who had supported the PKI, and this group came to constitute an important base of Golkar support.

Golkar's links with the military were also used to insure the allegiance of village heads. In some villages, particularly those that were former strongholds of the PKI, noncommissioned officers were installed as village heads. Another tactic was uncovered by Ward in his study of the 1971 elections in East Java:

> It was common practice in 1966–67 for *lurahs* (village heads) accused of Old Order sympathies to be dismissed as a result of strenuous protests made at the sub-district or regency levels by supporters of the New Order in the villages of East Java. *Resolusi* (resolutions) for the replacement of *lurahs* were also delivered when corruption and inefficiency were demonstrable. Party informants assured me that only party branches were influential enough to have a resolution accepted by the sub-district head. Appropriately, immunity to resolutions was one of the guarantees given to *lurahs* by Koramil (sub-district army command) representatives proselytizing on Golkar's behalf. In northern sub-districts of Kediri, for example, Koramils were wont to assure *lurahs*, even errant *lurahs*, that they would no longer have cause to worry about resolutions: "In fact, the more often they *kena resolusi* (are the target of resolutions), the more highly regarded will Golkar *lurahs* be." (1974: 191)

In general, as Ward observes, Golkar's efforts to destroy the influence of political parties did not entail the development of a new ideology. Instead, Golkar activists "simply endeavored to restore villagers to the traditionalist influence of rural and higher officialdom, with its military-reinforced power" (1974: 176).

Soon after the election, this principle found open expression in the official doctrine of the "floating mass." According to this doctrine, villagers should not be distracted from the tasks of economic development by political activity and, in order to ensure such single-minded concentration, all party branches below the regency level were closed down. Henceforth, as Ward observes: "The floating mass of villagers would remain under the *pembinaan* [guidance] of *lurahs*, Koramil commands and local police officials who would all, presumably, reactivate Golkar branches some time before the next election" (1974: 190).

Although the specific effects of village-level depoliticization on local power structures must have varied widely among villages, the implementation of the "floating mass" concept is part of the general process through which dominant rural groups have been transformed into clients of the state. In the course of becoming less subject to political pressures from within the village, these groups have become more reliant on supravillage authorities for their position and more susceptible to control by the state apparatus. At the same time, they have been the recipients of substantial state largesse.

These processes have been formalized and entrenched by two recent administrative reforms. First, the village assembly (*Lembaga Sosial Desa* or LSD) was replaced by a body known as the *Lembaga Ketahanan Masyarakat Desa* (LKMD). The chief significance of this transition is that in the past the leadership of the LSD was a nongovernmental position, whereas the village head is now leader of the LKMD. Evidence from Sukodono (discussed in chapter 4) shows how the LSD constituted a platform—albeit it rather limited—from which political struggles could be waged and which for a brief period facilitated the mobilization of popular support. By invoking "traditional" values of *musyawarah* (consultation) and *mufakat* (consensus), the LKMD seems designed to ensure that the masses continue to float.

The second change is that in some areas the village head and five village government officials have been appointed as civil servants (*pegawai negeri*) at the lowest level. This shift is extremely significant, because it means in effect that the political connections of village leadership within rural society have been almost totally severed. Village government officials are neither accountable to other villagers, nor can they use political support to strengthen their positions vis-à-vis the state.

Rice Policy Under the New Order

In addition to maintaining control over the rural sector, the New Order is vitally concerned with rice production and procurement. Rice is and always has been a critical determinant of the stability of the political-economic system. The state's need to ensure domestic procurement is underlined by the fragility of the international rice market, and dependence on foreign sources of rice has consistently been viewed as extremely risky, even with rapidly expanding oil revenues. New technologies in rice production became widely available in the late 1960s, and a huge proportion of the resources allocated to the rural sector have been aimed at increasing rice production. Indeed, the chief criticism of agricultural policy has been the neglect of nonrice crops (Falcon et al. 1984).

Rice policy has undergone substantial changes over the course of the New Order. On the face of it these changes have been in the direction of growing concessions, particularly to surplus producers. These concessions are not, however, simply a reflection of the pressure of increasingly powerful rural groups on the policy process. Instead, they seem to stem from the state's recognizing the limitations of a coercive approach to rice production and procurement, and antagonistic relations with the rural elite. This shift toward a more accommodative strategy in conjunction with the cooptation of the rural elite has been greatly facilitated by expanding oil revenues and is clearly reflected in three sets of policies: the Bimas package program, the rice price policy, and the formation of rural cooperatives.

The subordinate position of the rural sector as a whole in the early phases of the New Order is clearly evident in the coercive measures that the state initially used in its efforts to increase rice production and procurement (Hansen 1973). The notorious Bimas Gotong Royong program instituted early in 1969 involved several large European and Japanese chemical firms who contracted to provide fertilizer and pesticides on short-term credit and to assist in input distribution. All producers in the target areas were forced to use the inputs and to hand over to the state one-sixth of their harvest. Output even declined in some of these areas, particularly where irrigation facilities were inadequate and soils unsuitable. Also input deliveries were frequently late, and the aerial spraying of pesticides caused major ecological damage. The sliding repayment schedule did, however, provide farmers with a means of evasion, particularly because the bureaucracy was overextended. The government then decreed fixed cash repayment of credit. Unable to resist openly, farmers resorted to not using the inputs or to selling them on the black market. Noncompliance was most overt in western Java, where several districts withdrew from the program in 1970.

The "perfected" Bimas program introduced shortly thereafter recognized the limitations of outright coercion and relied more heavily on inducements. The main thrust of the program was an appeal to individual incentive. Farmers were permitted some discretion over the contents of the input package, although the state imposed maximum and minimum constraints. The block credit system of Bimas Gotong Royong was replaced with individual bank loans at 1 percent per month for seven months, which imposed fairly stringent minimum requirements for irrigation and farm size. The credit program is administered by the village units of Bank Rakyat Indonesia and technically bypasses village leadership. In practice, however, loans are generally granted on the recommendation of the village head.

Commenting on this type of phenomenon, Schulte-Nordholt (1978) points out that the cooperation of the *lurah* (village headman) is usually a decisive determinant of the "success" of government programs. Although the elimination of political activity at the village level makes organized opposition to the state virtually impossible, "projects which might threaten the village head's power and that of his family can be easily sabotaged by him; [conversely] . . . projects aimed at the economically strong farmers he can use to his full advantage" (Schulte-Nordholt 1978: 16).

Changes in price policy constitute the second element in the shift from thinly veiled coercion to accommodation. Rice prices and procurement have long been a major source of conflict between Javanese peasants and the state. By establishing a guaranteed floor price for rice and a ceiling price for fertilizer, the perfected Bimas program reflected an attempt by the state to resolve this conflict. Price and procurement measures worked reasonably well in 1970 and 1971, when good weather and improved input distribution and credit policies resulted in ex-

panded production. A severe drought in 1972 drastically reduced output, and rice prices rose sharply despite massive
imports of rice. In a determined move to increase stocks, the
government hastily expanded the newly instituted rural cooperatives and instructed them to purchase at least 10 percent of
the crop at a floor price substantially below the market price.
In some areas, the army was brought in to enforce the order,
and there were reports of peasants having to sell property and
possessions to meet the requirement in cash.

Since then the state has adopted an increasingly conciliatory
approach to price policy and procurement. Between 1973 and
1979, the floor price for rice in Java was increased by 211 percent (from Rp 45 to Rp 140 per kg) while the rise in ceiling
prices for both rice and fertilizer was considerably lower—from
Rp 100 to Rp 155 per kg (55 percent) for rice and 75 percent
for urea (Mears and Moeljono 1981: 43). During the second oil
boom (1979–1982), massive fertilizer subsidies together with
steadily rising farm gate prices generated even more favorable
price ratios (Dick 1982).

Rice price and procurement policy needs to be viewed in the
context of the system of cooperatives known as KUDs (*koperasi
unit desa* or village unit cooperatives), which were established in
1973. Despite the name, KUDs are in practice *kecamatan* (subdistrict)-based units and are supervised by a board chaired by
the *camat* (head of the subdistrict). There are now over 4,000
KUDs to about 300 *kecamatan,* or an average of 1 KUD to each
14 villages (Daroesman 1981: 24). Membership averages 350
people per KUD and is, not unexpectedly, composed primarily
of the landowning elite.

The changing functions of the KUD are a prime example of
the shifts in the state's stance toward the rural sector over the
course of the New Order. Initially the KUDs were formed in
order to assist the state in rice procurement. During the rice
shortge of 1973, the KUDs were expanded and pressed into
action on behalf of Bulog (*Badan Urusan Logistik,* the state rice
procurement agency) in ways that were contrary to the interests
of all rice producers. As rice price and procurement policy have
become more conciliatory, so too membership in the KUD has
come to offer growing material benefits. The procurement pro-

cess, initially a source of tension, is a key instance. The KUDs are provided with government credit in order to defend the floor price and are in principle obliged to purchase rice at no less than the official floor price. In practice, according to Dick (1979, 1982), the farm-gate prices received by most producers are below the floor prices paid by the KUD, and "the effect of the floor prices is . . . to pass back some of the benefits of the subsidy—the main beneficiaries are urban consumers—to those who can gain access to the KUD" (Dick 1982: 31).

The reasons for lower farm-gate prices have to do with poor rice quality, as well as the arrangements through which farmers are obliged to dispose of their crop to those from whom they have borrowed money. In addition, as Dick observes, Bulog purchases only 20 to 25 percent of the marketed rice crop, and this does not provide it with sufficient monopsony power to maintain the farm-gate price at the level of the floor price. Instead, given the retail price determined by Bulog's open market operations, the farm-gate price is determined by margins in private marketing channels. Because a smaller proportion of private margins are absorbed by subsidy, these margins are higher than those in Bulog's marketing channels and the farm-gate price is therefore lower. For a number of reasons, it is often neither possible nor practical for farmers to sell directly to the KUDs: "In these ways, opportunities are created for traders, who are often at the same time large farmers, truck owners, rice mill owners and village leaders, the emerging *kulak* class, to buy rice from farmers at harvest time and later resell it to the KUD at the higher floor price" (Dick 1982: 31).

Over time the functions of the KUD have become increasingly diversified. Between 1973 and 1976, a period in which fertilizer supplies were relatively scarce, the KUDs assumed control over fertilizer distribution (Mears and Moeljano 1981: 39). They were also provided with subsidized credit for the purchase of rice mills and, in some instances, tractors (Sinaga 1978). More recently, their functions were expanded to include the maintenance of floor prices for maize, soybeans, peanuts, mung beans, cloves, chickens, and eggs. In addition they administer *candak kulak* (traders') credit, a highly subsidized system of credit that seldom extends beyond a privileged few.

Since 1981–1982, the KUDs are charged with dealing with all sugarcane operations. Further, it appears that the state envisages an even wider range of activities for the KUDs in the future: "Although opinion in government is far from monolithic on this issue, there does seem to be a firming towards a policy of all 'basic needs' being distributed through the local cooperatives—this refers not only to rice and fertilizer, but also to most other farm or small-holder crops, to kerosene, and even in some cases to rural electrification" (Daroesman 1981: 23).

The expansion and diversification of the KUDs embodies the central features of the New Order's agrarian strategy. On the one hand, the KUDs provide an institutional framework within which the state can observe and control the rural elite. On the other hand, they are a medium for dispensing patronage to strategic rural groups, who are thereby more likely to identify their interests with those of the state. Accordingly, the KUDs control the rural elite, while at the same time they offer access to opportunities for accumulation.

CONCLUSION

In tracing the ways in which political-economic forces at the national level have both acted upon and been shaped by changing agrarian relations in the past, I have offered an alternative to the standard view that ecology and technology are the primary determinants of Javanese agrarian structure. The portrayal of the distinctive character of the contemporary Javanese rural elite and their clientist relationship to the state apparatus that emerges from this analysis is central to understanding the contemporary processes of agrarian change.

3

THE STRUCTURAL
TRANSFORMATION OF THE
INDONESIAN ECONOMY

The preceding chapter drew attention to some important similarities between the ways in which the New Order deals with the rural sector and the methods employed by the colonial state. These similarities stem primarily from an overriding desire to maintain control over the agrarian system, and the chief tactic in both instances has been the cooptation of strategic rural groups.

There is, however, a profound difference between the colonial state and the New Order—oil. The extractive motive, which was the raison d'être of colonial agrarian policy, has assumed an entirely different form in contemporary Indonesia. Although the New Order is still concerned about ensuring rice procurement, expanding oil revenues have made net extraction from the rural sector increasingly unnecessary and simultaneously have facilitated the shift from coercion to the more conciliatory modes of control described in the preceding chapter.

The state's access to external resources has also enabled it to extend and reinforce its control over other spheres of the economy, generating in the process some rather distinctive patterns of economic growth. In addition, significant shifts in macroeconomic policy and practices have taken place over the course of the New Order that in certain ways appear to move in the opposite direction from those that directly affect the rural sector.

PHASES OF MACROECONOMIC POLICY
UNDER THE NEW ORDER

Viewing the New Order as an institution that operates in part according to internal imperatives of preservation and aggran-

dizement (Anderson 1983) helps to highlight the crucial importance of the state's access to and control over resources. Rapidly
increasing oil revenues over the course of the New Order (table
1) have enabled the state to redefine the institutional arrangements that connect it to foreign and domestic capital. These
arrangements have in turn played a major role in shaping aggregate patterns of resource allocation and employment generation.

Macroeconomic policy under the New Order can usefully be
divided into three broad phases: An initial period of stabilization (1966–1972); the first oil boom (1973–1978); and the second oil boom (1979–1982).

Phase 1: 1966–1972

The overriding concern of the New Order when it first at-
tained power was to bring inflation under control in order to
stabilize the economy and also "to reconstitute the discipline,
cohesion, efficacy, and power of officialdom" (Anderson 1983:
488). For the same reasons, the state was desperately in need of
access to foreign resources: "The apparatus had to be provided
with a *stable* hierarchy of emoluments, and at a sufficient level
to command a unified subordination and loyalty" (ibid.). Measures designed to mobilize Western and Japanese aid and investment were extraordinarily successful, and government revenues from these sources rose sharply during this period.

Although there was considerable opening up of the economy
to external influences, the state continued to play a major role
in the economy. In particular, the military retained control over
strategic sectors (notably rice, oil, lumber, and other extractive
industries) to which they had gained access under Sukarno,
and continued to run them as fiefdoms rather than publicly
accountable state enterprises (Robison 1978). The dominance
of state enterprises was, however, quickly eclipsed by foreign
investment, the growth of which caused a precipitous decline
in the position of indigenous entrepreneurs in commerce and
industry. This group, a primarily orthodox Muslim bourgeoisie
concentrated in small-scale trade and manufacturing, had long
occupied a rather peripheral position (Robison 1978).

According to one view, the Indonesian state is in the contra-

TABLE 1. Government Revenues and Expenditures, 1969–1982

	Revenues				Expenditures	
	TOTAL (RP. BILLION)	OIL (% SHARE)	AID (% SHARE)	REVENUE/ GDP	TOTAL (RP. BILLION)	EXPENDITURE/ GDP
1969–1970	334.7	20	27	12.3	309.4	11.4
1970–1971	465.0	21	26	14.7	416.3	12.9
1971–1972	563.5	25	24	15.3	500.0	13.6
1972–1973	748.4	31	21	16.4	674.0	14.8
1973–1974	1,171.6	33	17	17.3	1,050.1	15.5
1974–1975	1,985.7	48	12	18.5	1,782.0	16.6
1975–1976	2,733.5	46	18	21.6	2,258.9	17.9
1976–1977	3,689.8	44	21	23.9	2,910.7	18.8
1977–1978	4,308.8	45	18	22.6	3,568.1	18.7
1978–1979	5,301.6	44	20	23.3	4,312.0	19.0
1979–1980	8,077.9	53	17	25.2	6,759.7	21.1
1980–1981	11,720.8	60	13	25.8	10,286.4	22.6
1981–1982	13,921.6	62	12	25.9	12,253.8	22.8
1982–1983	15,607.3	58	12	n.a.	13,781.6	n.a.

Source: Republik Indonesia, 1983–1984.
Note: The exchange rate was U.S. $1 = Rp 415 until November 1978 and Rp 625 thereafter.

dictory position of trying simultaneously to serve the interests of foreign capital and domestic capital. The strategically stronger position of foreign capital increasingly circumscribes the extent to which the state can undertake measures to improve the situation of indigenous capitalists. This in turn "brings the state progressively closer to a complete accommodation of imperialist interests" (Short 1979: 153).

A different and far more illuminating view of the links between foreign and domestic capital is to be found in Anderson's analysis of the peculiar nature of the New Order state (1983). Anderson observes that the advantages that multinational interests offer the state far outweigh the domestic resentments to which they give rise. They provide the center with sizable and reliable revenues, but, most important, they do not pose the direct political threat that a powerful indigenous capitalist class would do. By the same token, "indigenous entrepreneurial elements ravaged from one side by the multinationals *may* profit handsomely from another side—but only by grace of the state. They may prosper, but this prosperity cannot form the basis of any challenge to officialdom" (Anderson 1983: 490).

The state's position vis-à-vis the class of small indigenous entrepreneurs was, therefore, not so much one of being constrained in assisting them; rather, this class was becoming both politically and economically irrelevant. Not only were the spheres of manufacture in which they had previously held sway rapidly taken over by more advanced capital and technology, but, as the state gained access to external resources, it dissolved the anticommunist coalition that had formed the entrepreneurs' original base of support (Anderson 1983). A part of this initial coalition, the Muslim merchant bourgeoisie were rendered superfluous.

This process of dispensing with petty capitalists in trade and manufacture stands in sharp contrast to the way in which the state's interests in the rural elite were developing. During this period, the state was becoming increasingly aware of the need for making concessions to surplus rice producers in order to ensure production and procurement. At the same time, the "departyization" and control of the countryside described in chapter 2 required that strategic rural groups be incorporated under the Golkar umbrella and rewarded accordingly.

Phase 2: 1973–1978

Although the major growth in oil revenues took place after 1973–1974, the growing importance of oil was apparent several years earlier (table 1). The central feature of policy during the first oil boom was a proliferation of bureaucratic controls, a tendency that elicited severe criticism from many economists and donors (Booth and McCawley 1981; Glassburner 1978; Paauw 1979). Opinions differ over such questions as the feasibility of a labor-intensive, export-led growth pattern and the implications of high levels of oil revenues for short- and long-term investment strategy. There is, nevertheless, widespread agreement that many economic policies and procedures have tended to stifle investment, to distort it in an excessively capital-intensive direction, and to result in a great deal of unproductive investment. Particular criticism has been levelled against investment review, licensing procedures, import controls, and a wide range of other measures, such as subsidized credit, that have lowered the price of capital. Frequent implications are that these policies are simply misguided or that they form the basis for extensive corruption, and that the interests of almost all Indonesians would be better served by policies embodying more rational economic principles and greater reliance on market mechanisms.

What many critics often fail to take into account is that the measures that they view as uniformly counterproductive are often the key mechanisms for maintaining and consolidating the highly centralized power structure. A prime example is the Foreign Capital Investment Law of 1967, which opened the economy to foreign investment and which was amended in 1974 to include a number of new regulations. The new regulations included stipulations on the share of Indonesian capital in manufacturing profits; requirements that new ventures could only be undertaken together with the government, with *pribumi* (indigenous), or with *pribumi*-dominated corporate partnerships (Donges et al. 1980: 394); limited investment incentives to certain "priority" projects; and closed several branches to further foreign investment.

In practice, several provisions of the amended law constitute bases for alliances between multinationals and senior bureaucrats or military officials in which access to markets and resources is exchanged for a share of the product. Meticulous documentation of such alliances is provided by Robison, who shows how these arrangements operate through direct ties between particular centers of politicobureaucratic power and multinationals rather than through public policy channels (1978). Precisely because the system is contingent on the exercise of bureaucratic control over economic concessions, it generates highly interventionist policies. These concessions are important not only in extractive sectors, but also in spheres of manufacturing, such as motor car assembly, where value added often seems to be negative (Paauw 1979).

The state's relations with domestic capital came to be governed by a similar set of mechanisms over this period. Despite considerable rhetoric surrounding the development of *pribumi* enterprise, policy was in effect directed toward ensuring that accumulation by domestic entrepreneurs took place under the auspices of state patronage. This strategy gave rise to a small group of what Robison terms *asli* (indigenous) client capitalists; he points to their extremely precarious position, which hinged almost entirely on personal connections to patrons within the state apparatus. The inherent insecurity of these relationships in turn tended to bias investment toward short-term speculative gain; indeed, Robison found that many of the *asli* clients did not undertake any direct investment at all but acted primarily as contract brokers (1978: 36–37).

In these and other ways, the state moved to consolidate its position and restructure its relationship with both foreign and domestic capital, and oil revenues played a major role in this process. The chief consequence was a highly concentrated pattern of aggregate resource allocation and very little incremental employment generation. Although these investment patterns are partly inherent to the nature of oil-led growth, they need to be seen in the context of the increasingly centralized power structure that evolved over this period.

Phase 3: 1979–1982

Toward the end of 1978, Indonesian policy makers and their advisors were expressing considerable concern over the prospect of declining oil revenues. The 50 percent devaluation of the rupiah in November 1978 was a response to these concerns. Devaluation is primarily a fiscal device that allowed the government to increase domestic expenditure while continuing to balance the budget. Because the government is the largest seller of foreign exchange, it is, therefore, the major beneficiary of devaluation (Scherer 1982: 18).

Although annual oil production declined from 580 to 577 million barrels between 1979 and 1982, sharply increasing oil prices resulted in massive increases in government revenues during this period (table 1). Growing revenues were matched by large increases in expenditure, which, together with several years of bumper rice crops, fuelled a major upsurge in economic activity. The second oil boom also coincided with the launching of the third five-year plan (Repelita III), which was accompanied by a great deal of rhetoric about the "equitable distribution of the fruits of development."[1]

On the face of it, the broad sectoral allocation of resources remained more or less unchanged after 1979, except for a notable increase in the share of "government apparatus" (McCawley 1983). However, the huge absolute increases in government spending were associated with efforts to channel resources into previously neglected sectors of the economy.

Decentralization of the development budget—at least in absolute terms—is one of the important changes after 1979. There was, for instance, a sharp increase in the volume of development expenditures channeled directly to provincial, regency, and village governments instead of to central department branches in the region (Daroesman 1981; *Republik Indonesia* 1983–1984). This program, known as Inpres (an acronym for Presidential Instruction) also covers direct grants for the construction of primary school buildings, health infrastructure, road repair, and regreening. Indeed, the second oil boom was manifest primarily as a boom in construction.

Other examples of greater decentralization are a series of Provincial Development Programs (PDP) launched on an ex-

---

1. Although difficult to document, it seems likely that the state's greater attention to questions of equity was a reflection both of external pressure and of concern over the consequences of highly skewed patterns of growth following the first oil boom.

perimental basis since 1979. These programs, funded mainly by American and West German sources, are "designed to reach the rural poor through credit, employment, industrial and other programs, to develop greater capability in planning and executing programs at the provincial and *kabupaten* (regency) levels, and to increase the capability of central government agencies to support the development of local government" (Daroesman 1981: 16).

Accompanying these more decentralized patterns of spending was a series of presidential decrees (Keppres) requiring that preference be given in the allocation of government contracts to "weak economic groups," defined as those with at least 50 percent indigenous ownership and net assets not exceeding Rp 25 million in the case of trade and services, and Rp 100 million for industrial and construction enterprises. Local cooperatives, which in the rural sector means the KUDs discussed in chapter 2, also qualify as "weak economic groups." Two medium- and long-term credit programs offering highly subsidized interest rates were also established to assist these groups.

These programs have been the target of considerable criticism on the grounds that the use of financial policies to attain social objectives is ineffective and has constrained industrial growth. What is significant about these types of programs is that they reflect an effort by the state to extend its patronage base beyond the narrow group of *asli* client capitalists, which emerged during the first part of the 1970s, and they are analogous in certain ways to the rural cooperatives.

In general, an important shift in the state's position vis-à-vis Indonesian society and economy appears to have taken place in the late 1970s. It is important to bear in mind, however, that over this period the state was not only dispensing largesse more generously than before but was also using its enhanced position in order to regulate even more closely its relations with strategic groups. The village government reforms discussed in chapter 2 are a prime example of the way in which the state's growing ability to buy off certain groups was associated with tightening control over them.

TABLE 2. Sectoral Real Growth Rates, 1970–1981 (1973 constant prices)

	Agriculture, forestry, & fishing	Mining	Industry	Construction	Transport & communications	Trade & services	GDP
1970	4.1	15.5	9.0	25.4	4.4	8.7	7.5
1971	3.6	5.6	12.6	19.6	27.3	7.7	7.0
1972	1.6	22.3	15.1	29.8	9.0	13.0	9.4
1973	9.3	23.3	15.2	18.0	12.2	7.5	11.3
1974	3.7	3.4	16.2	22.1	12.1	9.2	7.6
1975	0	−3.6	12.3	14.0	5.1	10.7	5.0
1976	4.7	15.0	9.7	5.4	13.2	5.0	6.9
1977	1.3	12.4	13.7	20.6	28.1	10.3	8.9
1978	5.1	−2.0	16.8	14.0	17.2	8.0	7.7
1979	3.9	−0.2	12.9	6.4	8.9	7.5	6.3
1980	5.2	−1.2	22.2	13.6	8.9	12.3	9.9
1981	3.5	3.3	12.0	9.6	7.1	10.1	7.6
Average, 1970–1981	3.8	6.7	14.4	15.5	13.3	9.2	7.9

Source: Republik Indonesia, 1983–1984

TRENDS IN GROWTH, EMPLOYMENT, AND INCOME DISTRIBUTION

Patterns of Economic Growth and Structural Change

The rapid growth and structural transformation of the Indonesian economy under the New Order are clearly portrayed in tables 2 and 3. The declining relative importance of the agricultural sector conforms to the usual pattern of structural change in the context of rapid growth, but, in several other

TABLE 3. Percentage Changes in Sectoral Output Shares, 1960–1981

Sector	1960	1967	1971	1978	1981
Current Prices					
Agriculture	53.9	54.0	44.8	29.5	24.5
Mining	3.7	2.7	8.0	19.2	24.2
Industry & utilities	8.4	7.3	8.9	11.1	12.2
Construction, transport, & communications	2.0	1.7	3.5	5.5	5.6
Trade, finance, &			4.4	4.5	4.1
other services	32.0	34.3	30.4	30.2	29.4
	100	100	100	100	100
Constant Prices[a]					
Agriculture	53.9	51.8	44.0	32.8	29.5
Mining	3.7	3.7	9.9	11.0	8.9
Industry & utilities	8.4	8.4	9.3	13.5	16.7
Construction, transport, & communication	2.0	1.6	3.1	5.5	5.8
Trade, finance, &			3.8	5.4	51.4
other services	32.0	34.5	29.9	31.8	33.7
	100	100	100	100	100

Sources: 1960–67: Dapice 1980a; 1971–81: Republik Indonesia 1983–1984.
[a] 1960–1967: 1960 constant prices; 1971–1981: 1973 constant prices

respects, the Indonesian case is unusual. Most notably, industrial growth has been very slow, both when compared to other countries with similar rates of GDP growth and relative to the resources allocated to the industrial sector (McCawley 1981). In terms of both growth and employment generation, the construction and transport/communications sectors have performed far better.

Shifts in sectoral shares are much larger when valued in current rather than in constant prices because the latter remove the effect of higher oil prices. Indeed, the discrepancy between the two measures is largely a reflection of the impact of oil on the structure of the economy. At the same time, the data in tables 2 and 3 show that economic growth was not simply the *direct consequence of expanding oil revenues.* Growth of GDP had accelerated prior to the first oil boom, and real GDP continued to grow after 1979 when the physical volume of oil production and exports stagnated and then fell. Although the relative importance of the agricultural sector has declined, agricultural expansion is still the chief component of overall real growth. In the early phases of the New Order, the growth of nonfood crops—particularly lumber—was a significant source of growth and foreign exchange. In the late 1970s and early 1980s, rice production grew very rapidly. To the extent that oil revenues financed the heavy subsidies to rice production, oil contributed indirectly to the rapid growth of the rice sector and, given the weight of this sector, to the economy as a whole.

The Shifting Structure of Employment

Employment data derived from censuses and surveys are notoriously difficult to interpret because the standard concepts of employment on which they are based fail to capture some important aspects of work organization (Myrdal 1967; Connell and Lipton 1977). The chief problem is that a great deal of labor takes place outside a wage nexus and the criteria for what constitutes "employment" are therefore often vague. Further, a key feature of work organization in Java is extreme occupational multiplicity (White 1979). People derive their livelihood from a variety of different sources; these sources vary seasonally and also include a range of different types of work within a single day. In principle, it should nevertheless be possible to use national employment data to trace changes over time. The main problem with using the Indonesian data for this purpose is that the reference period has varied substantially among censuses and surveys.[2]

The question of whether economic growth has been accompanied by growing employment is one of the many that depend critically on definition. When intercensal survey data (SUPAS) became available in 1976, they seemed to show substantial increases in labor force participation rates since the 1971 census, particularly among women. Subsequent labor force surveys (SAKERNAS), which have been conducted every quarter since the end of 1976, and the 1980 census suggest that the SUPAS measures of labor force participation rates are inflated relative to other measures. One explanation is that SUPAS included as labor force participants unpaid family workers—mainly women and children—that other surveys did not (Arndt and Sundrum 1980). In addition, the SUPAS survey was conducted at the peak of the main rice harvest in 1976 (Strout 1983). According to the census data, employment in Indonesia as a whole increased by 2.9 percent a year over the 1970s (table 4), considerably below the 4.7 percent suggested by the intercensal data for the first part of the 1970s. Strout argues that the census estimate is too low, and that the figure is probably closer to 3.5 percent (ibid.).

The relatively slow growth of agricultural employment since 1961 is, of course, consistent with the steady decline in the proportion of the work force in agriculture (table 4). Jones notes, however, that the decline of nearly 10 percent between 1961 and 1971 could in large part reflect the longer reference period used in the 1961 census (1981). Particularly if nonagricultural activities are considered inferior to those in agriculture, a person is more likely to identify him or herself as an agricultural worker when asked about longer-term activities. Others argue that the continuing decline in the proportion of the work force

2. The reference period for what constitutes "working" has become progressively shorter (Scherer, 1982: 27). As explained below, these shifts could form part of the explanation for apparent changes in the structure of employment.

TABLE 4. Employment Growth by Sector, 1971–1980

	Sectoral shares			Annual percentage increase	Share of total increase	Annual percentage growth in output per worker
	1961	1971	1980	1971–1980	1971–1980	1971–1980
Agriculture	73.6	65.9	55.5	1.0	20.6	2.9
Mining		0.2	0.7	16.5	2.4	–13.8
Manufacturing	7.8	7.8	8.6	4.1	11.5	9.3
Utilities		0.1	0.2	8.9	0.4	4.2
Construction	8.9	2.0	3.1	8.4	7.0	6.6
Transport & communications		2.4	2.9	5.0	4.5	6.9
Trade		10.9	12.1	5.0	20.4	1.3
Finance	9.7	0.3	0.5	10.1	1.2	3.4
Services		10.4	15.4	7.5	32.1	1.7
Total	100	100	100	2.9	100	4.8

Source: Scherer 1982.

in agriculture indicated by the intercensal surveys since 1971 may be similarly illusory, given that these surveys used even shorter reference periods than the 1971 census (Abey, Booth, and Sundrum 1981). Preliminary analysis of the 1980 census data suggests, however, that the falling share of agriculture in total employment over the 1970s is not simply a distortion caused by definitional changes. Scherer shows that bringing the 1980 estimates into line with the 1971 census by eliminating those who worked only one day a week in 1980 has virtually no effect (1982).

The growing relative importance of nonagricultural activities suggested by the macro data forms the core of much of the debate over whether or not poorer groups benefitted from rapid growth over the first part of the 1970s. The key issue is whether people were being pulled into activities generated by overall economic expansion or whether they were being pushed out of agriculture into inferior activities. The labor force surveys and censuses contain little information that could be used to address these questions, and efforts to interpret the data on employment trends have had to rely heavily on indirect evidence and some fairly strong assumptions.

One point that is reasonably clear is that the shift of the work force out of agriculture cannot be explained simply in terms of rural-urban migration. A consistent finding of the surveys and censuses is that the proportion of the population in rural areas remained virtually unchanged through most of the 1970s— about 80 percent. This figure needs to be tempered with the recognition that population densities in Java are such that rural-urban distinctions are often meaningless. Also, municipal definitions remained unchanged until the 1980 census and therefore fail to take account of urban agglomeration, which is probably considerable in some areas. Despite these and other caveats about the accuracy of the macro data on population distribution, it seems to be the case that rural-urban migration in Java was comparatively low over much of the 1970s (Speare 1981). This pattern is particularly remarkable in view of the rapid growth of the economy as a whole, and some of the possible reasons for it are discussed in chapter 8. The chief implication is that the expansion of nonagricultural activities—at least during the first part of the 1970s—was primarily an agrarian phenomenon.

Although there is no precise survey information on the nature of these activities or the returns that they yield, the census data do indicate tremendous variations among sectors in average labor productivity (table 4) and also that the two lowest productivity sectors (trade and services) accounted for more than one-half the growth in employment. There are also enormous variations in productivity within sectors. According to the 1974–1975 industrial census, large and medium firms accounted for 13 percent of industrial workers and 80 percent of value added, while the shares of cottage industries were precisely the reverse (McCawley 1981: 68). Value added per worker ranged from Rp 721,000 in medium-large firms, to Rp 129,000 in small firms, to Rp 19,000 in cottage industries.

The composition of the industrial work force is highly revealing. About 80 percent of the manufacturing work force was located in rural areas and one-half were women; a large majority of these women were "own account workers" or "unpaid family workers," while most males were employed as wage laborers (McCawley 1981: 69). These data obviously reflect the dominance of the cottage industry, over 50 percent of which consisted of bamboo weaving and coconut sugar production. Micro studies conducted over the first part of the 1970s confirm that such activities offer extremely low returns, which were frequently below agricultural wages but provided a fairly constant stream of income. These studies, summarized by White (1979), reveal a range of other marginal activities in which people engage when they have no other options.

On a more aggregate level, Dapice's comparison of sectoral shares in employment and output over the first part of the 1970s indicates a pattern of large productivity gains in a very limited set of "modern" sector activities along with a huge proportion of the work force engaged in very low productivity activities (1980b).[3]

3. Papanek shows that apparent increases in industrial wages are primarily attributable to a shift to more capital and to skill-intensive types of firms: "The increase of 68 percent in the real industrial wage between 1970 and 1977 seems to reflect more an increase in the dualistic structure of industry than an increase in the income of the broad mass of unskilled workers" (1980: 34).

Trends in Income Distribution and Level of Living

The employment data clearly raise more distributional questions than they are capable of answering. The Indonesian Central Bureau of Statistics conducted national expenditure surveys in 1970 and again in 1976; I shall examine the extent to which these surveys (known as SUSENAS, an acronym for national socioeconomic surveys) shed light on some important questions.

Bearing in mind that rural-urban distinctions in Java have become somewhat blurred, the SUSENAS surveys reveal, first, a striking pattern of growing rural-urban disparity. Average expenditure has grown significantly faster in urban than in rural areas, and a huge proportion of income growth is accounted for by Jakarta where growth in expenditure was more than 20 percent higher than in other urban areas in Java and 30 percent above the average for the country as a whole (Sundrum 1979). Booth and Sundrum estimate that, although Indonesia's rural-urban disparity in 1970 was one of the lowest in the sixteen countries for which data are available, it had increased by 1976—particularly in Java—to one of the highest (1981).

The conclusion usually drawn from the SUSENAS data is that the degree of inequality within urban areas increased, while that in rural areas narrowed slightly.[4] Dapice, however, shows that there is a substantial discrepancy between total spending calculated from the SUSENAS data and that indicated by the national accounts; he suggests that much of the shortfall is attributable to the underestimation of luxury consumption by the SUSENAS surveys (1980b). He points out that purchases of new cars and motorcycles alone account for 5 to 6 percent of total consumption, and that this, together with spending on foreign travel, gasoline, and expensive consumer

---

4. Sundrum (1979: 140) cites the following Gini coefficients:

	1970	1976
Java		
Urban	.3319	.3974
Jakarta	.3098	.3858
Rural	.2977	.2956
Outer Islands		
Urban	.3002	.3060
Rural	.3303	.2980

durables, is responsible for much of the discrepancy between the SUSENAS data and the national accounts. Because luxury consumption tends to be concentrated in the urban upper class, the extent of inequality between rural-urban areas and within urban areas is even greater than the SUSENAS data show, but it is clear that at least part of this luxury expenditure was by rural people, which casts doubt on the SUSENAS finding that intrarural disparities have narrowed (Booth and Sundrum 1981: 182).

The key question is, of course, whether or not the income of the rural poor rose during this period of rapid growth. Different analysts have arrived at totally different conclusions from the data. According to Leiserson et al., the real per capita income of the poorest 40 percent of the rural population rose between 3 and 5 percent per year between 1970 and 1976 (1978). Dapice, in contrast, concludes that the average real per capita income of the rural poor remained more or less stagnant (1980b). The reason for these differences lies in the method used to correct for the effects of inflation. The optimistic estimate is based on a set of standard price indices, while the pessimistic one is derived from an implicit price index that takes account of the consumption bundle specific to poor rural consumers (table 5). During the period under consideration, the prices of commodities consumed by the poor rose relatively rapidly, and their income gains were proportionately lower than those of other income groups.

Technology, Land Distribution, and Labor Use

The availability of staple foodgrains, together with the social and technological conditions under which they are produced, is central to any analysis of how the rural poor are faring. Total staple food availability from domestic production changed very little over most of the 1970s, in large part because of the stagnation of staple nonrice crops. After 1977 it rose dramatically, primarily as the consequence of several years of bumper rice crops; Dick estimates that total domestic food production per capita in rice equivalents rose from 174 kg in 1977 to 202 kg in 1980 (1982).

TABLE 5. Alternative Estimates of Real Per Capita Expenditure in Java, 1970–1976

	Per capita expenditure in current Rp.		Alternative price indices[a]			Alternative estimates of changes in real expenditure, 1970–1976		
	1970	1976	A	B	C	A	B	C
Total								
Urban	1714	7025	273	305	298	50.2%	34.4%	37.5%
Rural	1029	3468	284	304	329	18.7%	10.7%	2.4%
Poorest 40 percent								
Urban	828	3058	273	305	299	31.2%	19.2%	23.4%
Rural	541	1929	284	304	346	23.4%	16.2%	3.1%

Sources: Per capita nominal expenditure, 9 essential commodities index, and food price index from Leiserson et al. (1978); implicit SUSENAS prices from Dapice (1980b).

[a]Definitions: A = 9 essential commodities; B = food price index; and C = implicit SUSENAS prices.

In spite of pest infestations and other ecological problems associated with the dissemination of modern rice technology, rice production expanded fairly steadily over the first part of the 1970s. Between 1971 and 1978, the proportion of rice fields planted to modern rice varieties increased from 30 to 67 percent. Yields rose from 2.7 to 3.2 tons per ha compared with averages that fluctuated between 1.8 and 2.2 tons per ha between 1960 and 1967 (Bernsten et al. 1981). Despite a slight decline in the rice area harvested, the annual rate of growth of rice production averaged 3.6 percent (Mears and Moeljono 1981). After 1978 there were substantial increases in both area harvested and yield, and the average annual growth of rice production rose from 17.5 million tons in 1978 to 22.3 million tons in 1981 (Republik Indonesia 1983–1984: 257).

The most comprehensive national data on agricultural change are a set of agricultural surveys conducted annually by the Central Bureau of Statistics between 1968 and 1978 (Handoko et al. 1982). These surveys unfortunately contain virtually no information on demographic structure, asset ownership, nonagricultural income, and so forth, which would facilitate analysis of the relationships between socioeconomic status and resource use. The limited farm management data could in principle provide some insights into distributional questions, but the sample changed each year and the basis for selection is rather questionable. At best these data allow us to examine patterns of technology adoption and agricultural resource use across farm size groups. "Farm size" refers to area operated and, by incorporating several assumptions, can be roughly adjusted for land quality. The lack of any information on landownership and tenurial arrangements precludes a more comprehensive estimate of control over land.

Despite these and other caveats about the usefulness of farm size measures, several fairly clear patterns do emerge from the agricultural survey data for Java. First, there is a direct relationship between farm size and the extent of adoption of modern varieties, but the disparities are smaller than often supposed and average rates of adoption have been rapid among all groups. For instance, between 1976 and 1978, approximately 60 percent of rice crops on farms below 0.2 ha were planted with modern varieties compared with 80 to 84 percent on farms larger than 2 ha; comparative figures for 1971 are 17 percent and 24 percent for the smallest and largest groups, respectively. Second, the data also suggest a direct relationship between farm size and fertilizer use, but the differences are small and diminishing. As the smaller farms use more green and animal manure, the differences in nonlabor inputs across farm size groups appear negligible.

In spite of these similarities, the surveys reveal the classic inverse relationship between farm size and yields. The explanation lies in patterns of labor use; labor input per hectare on the smallest farms is almost twice that on the largest farms. These differences are not simply a reflection of better soil quality on smaller farms. On the contrary, although the measure of irrigation in the survey data is imperfect, it seems that larger farms tend to have a higher proportion of irrigated area.

Macro information on land distribution and tenurial relations in Indonesia is extremely scanty. The only sources are agricultural censuses conducted in 1963 and 1973, which contain some data on area operated, but none on ownership and little on tenurial arrangements. What these data show, as one would expect, are growing limitations on access to land. The censuses indicate a 3 percent decline in the area of smallholdings in Java, which, together with a 4.2 percent increase in the number of farms, resulted in a 7 percent decrease in average farm size from 0.7 ha to 0.66 ha. The decline in smallholding area was due primarily to the expansion of estates.

There are two further effective limitations on access to land that would not be reflected in the data (Booth and Sundrum 1981). First, a substantial amount of land that would otherwise be planted to food crops (generally rice) is taken over by the state-controlled sugar industry for sugar production, and the land requisitioned for sugar production is generally the most fertile and best irrigated. The second restriction on access to land is the institution of *bengkok,* whereby village government officials are given usufructuary rights over high-quality land in lieu of salary. It is generally supposed that *bengkok* land comprises 10 to 15 percent of cultivable area; however, there is evidence to suggest that in some areas of Central Java the proportion of land under *bengkok* may be as high as 18 to 30 percent (ibid.: 186).

The most striking reflection of shrinking access to land has been the rapid increase in landlessness. It is extremely difficult to arrive at an unambiguous measure of the level or increase in landlessness, but there is little doubt that they have both been high. The growth in the number of farms was considerably below the increase in the number of rural households, even taking account of the possible overestimation of the proportion of the population in the rural sector. Probably the best estimate of landlessness, that derived from the ratio of farms to total rural households, was about 40 percent in Java in the early 1970s (Booth and Sundrum 1981: 189). Village studies in the densely populated lowland areas of Java frequently report levels of landlessness considerably higher than this.

It appears from the agricultural census data that land distribution within the landholding group remained virtually unchanged; the Gini coefficients for Java are 0.434 and 0.433 for 1963 and 1973, respectively (accounted for by a slight decline in the share of the top quintile that was taken over by the middle two quintiles) (Booth and Sundrum 1981: 183). This apparent constancy in land distribution probably masks some important shifts in patterns of access to and control over land, however. One indication is provided by the sketchy data on tenancy, which show that the proportion of "wholly owned" farms increased from 59 to 73 percent, and that of "wholly owned" areas from 55 to 70 percent from 1963 to 1973. These results are particularly surprising in view of the considerable anecdotal evidence of land acquisition by urban people, which one would expect to result in an increase in rental and share tenancy arrangements; it is possible, however, that rural landowners are withdrawing land from tenancy more rapidly than urban landowners are renting it out (White 1979).

Changing patterns of control over land, which are not reflected in the data on area operated, could also be taking place through complex tenurial arrangements. For instance, one of the most common arrangements is that a landowner who has mortgaged all or part of his or her land may operate the entire area under a sharecropping agreement. Such a farm could well show up in the census data as "wholly owned," despite the fact that the landowner may only be receiving a third or so of the yield. In general, the extraordinary complexity of tenurial arrangements—often closely tied in with labor and credit and sensitive to changing rural conditions—mean that it is extremely hazardous to draw firm conclusions about land distribution from agricultural census data.

The question most commonly posed is whether technological change has tended to increase or decrease agricultural employment. Most agree that mechanization is generally labor displacing, except in instances where it breaks seasonal labor bottlenecks. In the case of Java, most mechanization in rice production has been in postharvest operations, notably the shift from hand-pounding of rice to small rice mills, which has displaced a huge amount of female labor (Collier et al. 1973; Timmer 1973). Also, the replacement of the finger knife (*ani-ani*) with the sickle is estimated to reduce harvesting labor requirements per hectare by as much as 60 percent (Collier et al. 1973). The extent of mechanization in preharvest activities seems generally quite low, although in some areas rotary weeders have taken hold (White 1979), and in the late 1970s the government made available highly subsidized credit for the purchase of padi tractors through the KUDs (Sinaga 1978).

Far less consensus exists over the employment implications of seed-fertilizer technology. The general view is that modern rice varieties tend to raise labor demand on a per crop basis because they require more intensive weeding, more fertilizer, water control, and so forth; also, the shorter growing period allows for multiple cropping in well-irrigated areas and thus contributes to substantial annual increases in labor demand. The counterargument often used in the context of Java is that the spread of modern rice technology has tended to reduce income-earning opportunities in agriculture. The rationale for the latter argument, discussed in chapter 1, is that the high level of purchased inputs associated with modern rice technology has set in motion a process of commercialization, which has in turn been applied to labor relations. The consequent shift from work and poverty sharing to more commercialized labor relations has placed a downward pressure on labor demand.

On the face of it, the labor data contained in the agricultural surveys support neither view. In the three years for which reasonably unambiguous labor data are available (1976–1978), there is essentially no difference in labor use per hectare between modern and local rice varieties. The amount of labor used in weeding does tend to be slightly higher for modern varieties, but this is outweighed by somewhat lower levels of labor use in other activities. To the extent that one can discern longer-term trends in labor use from the data, it seems that rice labor input per hectare in Java has remained virtually unchanged (Hart 1983). Multiple cropping of rice has increased by about 2 percent per year, but this is below the growth in labor force, which appears to have been in the vicinity of about 3 percent. The only fairly clear change revealed by the data is a tendency toward a substitution of family for hired labor on small farms, particularly for harvesting.

Comparable farm management data are not available for the period after 1978, but all indications are that the major increases in rice production in this period were associated not only with increases in the level of labor demand, but also with important shifts in the pattern of seasonality. The rise in agricultural labor demand was probably attributable to increasing cropping intensity rather than higher labor input on a per crop basis. Collier et al. (1982), for instance, report that the number of crops per year had risen in twenty of the twenty-six villages they surveyed and that in all but one village farmers had shifted to high-yielding, pest-resistant varieties that also have a shorter growing cycle than local varieties. In addition, the aggregate patterns of labor demand probably became far more sharply seasonal over this period than had been the case earlier.

A new extension program (Insus) introduced in 1979 requires synchronized planting and, though the coverage of this program is limited, it seems likely that farmers were generally aware of the importance of synchronized planting in controlling pests. The data needed to document changing patterns of seasonality are not available at present, but two highly experienced researchers at Agro-Economic Survey confirmed my own impression that there had been a marked shift toward synchronized planting in many areas. These changing patterns of seasonality were probably associated with important changes in the institutional arrangements governing labor use in agriculture, an understanding of which is crucial to interpreting wage data.

On the face of it, the wage data from the agricultural surveys suggest that the real wages bill per hectare remained virtually unchanged between 1971 and 1977, but that it increased somewhat in 1978 (Handoko et al. 1982). The second set of macro data on agricultural wages is a series of daily wage rates for three activities (hoeing, transplanting, and weeding) collected on a monthly basis since January 1976 by the Central Bureau of Statistics and reported by Scherer (1982). These data also show that real wages measured in terms of rice rose after 1978. If, however, a more comprehensive deflator is used, the rise in real wages after 1978 is lower and in some areas disappears altogether (Scherer 1982).

INTERPRETING THE MACRO DATA: ISSUES AND PROBLEMS

The paucity of data on rural nonagricultural activities has meant that the interpretation of shifts in the composition of rural employment over the first part of the 1970s rests on the question of whether or not rural labor markets operate competitively. Those who assume that labor markets are relatively competitive maintain that the declining growth of agricultural employment was offset by expanding nonagricultural opportunities, and that the move of labor out of agriculture was a healthy process of inducement. The rationale for this conclusion derives from the observation that real agricultural wages appear to have remained more or less constant. Assuming that labor markets operate competitively and, therefore, that returns to labor in nonagricultural activities must approximate "the" agricultural wage, proponents of this approach then conclude that "despite the relative decline in the demand for labor in Javanese agriculture ... the demand for labor in non-agricultural activities appears to have expanded sufficiently to avoid any general and substantial decline in real wages in Java," and that "the growth in overall employment levels must be interpreted as evidence of the widespread and substantial impact on the labor market of the rapid increases in output and investment in the first half of the decade" (Leiserson et al. 1978: 45, iii).

non-competitive views of labor markets

The alternative view is that there are mechanisms that prevent the availability of additional labor from bidding down wages. Although analyses of the mechanisms responsible for segmentation differ, this approach provides a basis for a far more pessimistic interpretation of the macro data. The key contrast with the competitive model lies in the explanation of expanding nonagricultural rural activities. In contrast to the competitive approach, which assumes this expansion to have been the consequence of outward shifts in the demand for labor, the segmentation model helps explain how a rise in the proportion of the work force engaged in nonagricultural activities along with constant agricultural wages is consistent with a "supply push" process whereby people who are excluded from agricultural jobs move into inferior nonagricultural activities in order to survive.

The obvious question posed by these two interpretations is how to distinguish between them, and the problem is that the macro data are incapable of doing so because of the paucity of disaggregated information on rural nonagricultural activities. In principle, the data on trends in levels of living of the rural poor over the first part of the 1970s are an indirect test, but we have seen how the results of these surveys are also ambiguous.

A potentially important pattern revealed by more recent analysis of the macro data is the shift in the structure of employment that seems to have occurred in the late 1970s. Table 6 shows an effort by Strout to interpolate census data with the labor force surveys (1983). This effort constitutes no more than a rough approximation, and considerable caution must be exercised in interpreting table 6. Bearing in mind these caveats, the results are interesting. They suggest that, until about 1977, agricultural employment grew slowly along with the remarkably rapid increases in nonagricultural employment. Thereafter, female agricultural employment expanded rapidly, but the growth of nonagricultural employment of both men and women slowed substantially.

This apparent slowdown in the growth of nonagricultural activities in the late 1970s and early 1980s underscores a major inconsistency in the neoclassical argument that people were being drawn out of agriculture by expanding nonagricultural activities over the first part of the 1970s.

According to the logic of the neoclassical interpretation, the relationship between agriculture and nonagriculture was reversed in the late 1970s and early 1980s when the growth in agricultural employment compensated for the slackening of nonagricultural jobs. The chief problem with this interpretation is that the Indonesian economy was booming in the late 1970s and early 1980s, and that the patterns of government expenditure that stimulated the boom generated more productive nonagricultural employment than had been the case in the past.

The apparent anomaly of the slackening growth of nonagricultural employment in the midst of a major boom disappears when one drops the assumption that nonagricultural jobs yield a homogeneous "wage" that approximates that in agriculture. A far more plausible interpretation is that significant changes

TABLE 6. Annual Rates of Employment Growth in Agriculture and Nonagriculture in Java

| | Labor force surveys | | Census |
	1971–1977	1977–1981	1971–1980
Agriculture			
Female	−2.44	5.50	0.66
Male	1.73	0.18	1.11
Both	0.26	2.02	0.97
Nonagriculture			
Female	7.51	4.90	6.46
Male	7.39	4.15	6.08
Both	7.43	4.43	6.22
Average	3.40	3.03	3.25

Source: Strout 1983.

in the composition of nonagricultural activities took place in the late 1970s. For men, this involved more productive jobs (particularly in construction and transport) and a decline in some of the marginal activities in which they had been involved earlier. Among women, the possible growth in the number of people gaining access to agricultural jobs as a consequence of greater seasonality may also have been associated with the reduction in more marginal nonagricultural activities, at least in peak periods of agricultural labor demand. The corollary, of course, is that a substantial part of the growth in nonagricultural activities during the first part of the 1970s reflected a process of marginalization.

This interpretation is consistent with the evidence reviewed above that showed that most of the incremental employment took place in segments of the economy in which the growth of output was slow. It is also closely in accord with analyses that have focussed on the highly capital-intensive and extractive growth pattern of the Indonesian economy over much of the 1970s.

Viewing trends in rural employment in this way raises a host of further questions. The most obvious are why, if indeed a growing reserve labor pool was developing during the 1970s, there did not appear to be a precipitous decline in wages and, conversely, why agricultural labor markets failed to clear. Beyond this issue are the more general questions of what are the processes and mechanisms of agrarian differentiation (of which the macro data are a reflection) and what are the forces that have shaped them.

It is towards gaining a better understanding of these issues that the case study that follows is devoted. Through a detailed examination of livelihood strategies in Sukodono in the mid-1970s, we shall see how the institutional arrangements that are taking shape operated so as to facilitate control over labor, while at the same time circumscribing the work opportunities available to some groups. Comparison of the findings from Sukodono with those of other micro studies reveals some essential similarities with labor arrangements in other parts of Java. This in-depth analysis sheds light on the internal logic of such arrangements, and on the economic and political conditions of which they are a reflection.

Part II
LABOR AND LIVELIHOOD IN SUKODONO

It must not be forgotten that when the countryside is poor, it takes little to create antagonistic social strata. Between the man who goes hungry, and the man who can satisfy his hunger, there is a world of difference, although, in economic terms, the difference may at times consist of a few dozen extra poods of grain or potatoes possessed by the more fortunate peasant.

M. Lewin,
Russian Peasants and Soviet Power

4

THE VILLAGE AND ITS PEOPLE

Sukodono is situated in the heart of one of the main rice-producing regions of Java, which was also subject to intense sugar cultivation during the colonial period (map 1). The heavy involvement of the village in colonial sugar production is indicated by a narrow-gauge railtrack (now defunct) that connects Sukodono to the local town. With its rich clay soils and well-developed irrigation facilities, Sukodono continues to be the target of externally imposed sugar production. Sukodono exemplifies clearly the similarities between colonial and contemporary policies discussed in chapter 2 and the contradictory nature of the relationship of the rural elite to the state apparatus.

METHODOLOGY

The Sukodono study formed part of the Project on the Ecology of Coastal Villages, a joint undertaking of the Indonesian Agro-Economic Survey (AES), Institut Pertanian Bogor (Bogor Agricultural University or IPB) and the Universitas Diponegoro in Semarang. In addition to studying the particular problems of Central Javanese coastal villages, the project was designed as a pilot study for the more extensive Rural Dynamics Study, which was subsequently undertaken by the Agro-Economic Survey in the Cimanuk Basin region of western Java. My role in the pilot study was twofold. First, I participated in setting up a computerized data management system and in training a group of data processors and computer programmers attached to the Agro-Economic Survey in Bogor who then went on to work with the Rural Dynamics Study. Second, I formulated a set of questionnaires that were subsequently adapted (and greatly improved) for use in that study. My affiliation with

79

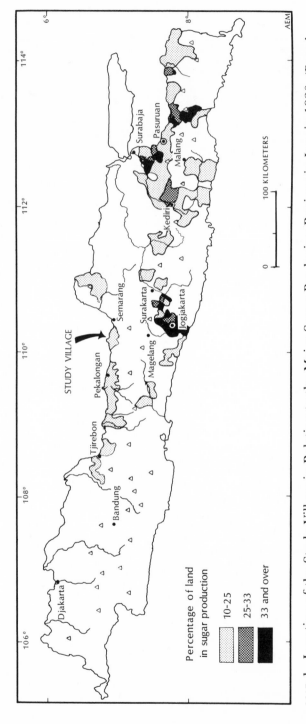

MAP 1. Location of the Study Village in Relation to the Major Sugar-Producing Regions in Java in 1920. (Based on C. Geertz, *Agricultural Involution: The Processes of Ecological Change in Indonesia*, Map 5.)

Agro-Economic Survey provided me with an unusual set of advantages in conducting field research but also constrained in certain ways the manner in which I collected and processed the data.

Chief among the advantages was that I had access to the extensive field experience of AES and IPB researchers and faculty. AES staff members had worked for some time in the three villages included in the ecology project, and they introduced me to village leaders and provided a great deal of background information. These introductions helped greatly in allaying initial suspicions—at least those of the village notables. Another enormous advantage was that I worked in the village in conjunction with a faculty member from IPB who had grown up in a Central Javanese village.

By participating in the project, I was constrained in the choice of village. From the three sample villages, I selected Sukodono because it is primarily a rice-cultivating village, whereas the other two are mainly fishing villages. Although brackish water fishponds are among the special features of Sukodono, it is fairly comparable with other rice-cultivating villages in Central Java in several important respects.

The main constraint stemmed from the distance of Sukodono from Bogor (a thirteen-hour drive) together with the AES requirements that I train personnel in Bogor and that all the raw data remain in Indonesia. In effect this meant that all the data had to be transferred to computer tapes and the data processing conducted in Bogor. To complicate matters further, the computer that we used was located in Jakarta (a one and a half to two-hour drive from Bogor with virtually no telephone communication) and was frequently in a state of collapse.

I dealt with these constraints by dividing my time between Sukodono and Bogor, which allowed me both to participate in field research and to oversee the data processing. At the same time, it meant that data collection was limited to the ten to twelve days each month that I was able to spend in the village. The method of collecting labor allocation data was dictated primarily by this restriction on my own time.

In Sukodono I lived in the house of the village headman (*lurah*). My social contact with poorer groups was limited by this association, as well as by language barriers. I speak and understand Bahasa Indonesia, the lingua franca of Indonesia, which in Sukodono at the time was understood only by the wealthier and more educated villagers. On a daily basis, people speak a north coast dialect of Javanese, a language quite distinct from Indonesian and considerably more complex. After many months in the village, I could follow a simple conversation in Javanese and could grasp the gist of an interview, but I did not become conversant in the language.

In addition to my linguistic limitations, the huge volume of detailed information necessitated a heavy reliance on interviewers. In recruiting interviewers, my colleague from IPB and I had in mind several critiera. First, the interviewers should be local people known to the villagers and likely to have their confidence. Second, they should not be people in positions of formal authority. Third, they should be willing and able to establish rapport with poor, low-status households.

In effect, the number of potential candidates was small because of the generally low level of education in the village. Some of the younger people had completed primary school and were reportedly eager for the job. Without exception, however, they were from the wealthiest class, and we were concerned about the way in which they would interact with poorer households. We were able to find only one suitable person from within the village, a teacher who taught in a secondary school about five km. away. The second interviewer was a teacher who lived in an adjacent village, a man from a comparatively low-status household who was well acquainted with many of the *orang kecil* ("little people") of Sukodono and who was by far the best of the three interviewers. I was particularly concerned that we hire at least one woman, but the only person we could find—a teacher in the village school who lived in the local town—proved almost completely incompetent. Because outright dismissal would have caused extreme embarrassment all round, we accepted her suggestion that we hire her husband in her place; though far from satisfactory, this compromise was less disruptive than any alternative.

The interviewers would arrive at the *pendopo* (porch) of the *lurah's* house which served as a makeshift office at about 2 P.M., and we would spend an hour or two going over the questionnaires from the day before, which I had spent the morning checking for consistency and completeness. Each interviewer would visit three households a day, between about 4 and 8 P.M., stopping at the *mahgreb* prayer time (6 to 6:30 P.M.). My colleague from IPB and I attended between a third and a half of the interviews. During my first three or four months in Sukodono, I attracted a large following of children, commenting at length and with great amusement on my size and strange appearance, and I soon became accustomed to being observed closely while working on the porch of the *lurah*'s house. This attention meant that my presence during interviews created a great deal of disturbance, but, by about my fifth or sixth month in Sukodono, the novelty of a comparatively large, pale, peculiarly clad woman going around the village had more or less worn off.

Particularly in the early stages, I was also observed closely by a village government official who had been instructed to ensure that I did not ask questions of a political nature or engage in any other form of political activity. He too eventually lost interest, particularly when I tried to engage him in activities like helping to measure plots, but the forces that he represented remained a palpable constraint.

My evenings were mostly spent chatting with members of the *lurah*'s family, his retainers and the family of his close political rival (the village secretary), who were frequent visitors during my stays in Sukodono and who also regularly invited me to their house. In retrospect I realize that the way in which I have interpreted the evidence has been shaped in important ways by these informal gatherings.

Sampling Design and Procedures

Our aim was to select a sample of households whose landholdings were representative of landholding patterns in the village as a whole, and a census of landholdings in Sukodono conducted by AES in 1974 constituted the sampling frame. Landowning households were stratified on the basis of rice land owned, and within each stratum a proportional sample was selected systematically. The census data on landownership of each household were listed in descending order according to residential block or *dukuh,* of which there are four. Landowning households living in a particular residential block are likely to own land in an adjacent area of the village. From the basic listings, separate lists were drawn up in which landowning households within each landowning size group were listed according to residential block, and the systematic sampling procedure was intended to ensure that all four blocks would be represented proportionately. Landless households were randomly selected after excluding households containing only one member.

Initially we selected a sample of eighty-seven households from which eleven replacements had to be made. Two of the originally selected households had left the village; in a third the household head had died, and the land was being operated by a relative. Three landowning households (all in the small to medium range) had either rented out or sold their land and were no longer operating any land at all. Accordingly, the evidence on loss of control over land discussed below probably understates the extent of this phenomenon in Sukodono. The other five households that were replaced were all fishpond-owning households; several of these denied fishpond ownership, and two others owned fishponds in another village and male members of the household were rarely at home. During the course of the survey, one household dropped out; this was an extremely orthodox Muslim household, the male members of which objected to the women being interviewed by men. In the second half of the survey, we decided that our resources allowed for expanding the sample, and an additional six households were added.

Table 7 summarizes landownership patterns in both the village population and the initial sample of eighty-six households. In the process of interviewing, we found that landholding sizes frequently differed from those reported in the census. As discussed below, landholding data proved the most difficult and complex to collect, and throughout our eighteen months' field research we were constantly revising this information. In part the discrepancies between the census and interview data on landholdings are attributable to changes that had taken place in the intervening year, a period marked by rather depressed

TABLE 7. Rice Landownership in the Population and Sample, Sukodono

	Rice land (ha)					Fishponds only	No rice land or fishponds
	≥1.0	.60–.99	.50–.59	.30–.49	≤.29		
Population							
No. of households	32	83	43	57	22	14	247
Households as % of pop.	6.4	16.7	8.6	11.4	4.4	2.8	49.7
Rice land owned as % of total	45.5	29.8	11.2	11.0	2.5		
Average area of rice land owned (ha)	2.77	0.69	0.51	0.38	.022		
Sample							
No. of households	7	7	11	12	7	2	40
Households as % of pop.	8.1	8.1	12.9	14.0	8.1	2.3	46.5
Rice land owned as % of total	51.1	14.4	17.5	12.8	4.2		
Average area of rice land owned (ha)	2.56	0.72	0.56	0.37	.021		

conditions. In many instances, however, they are due to the problems inherent in collecting these types of data. The general tendency seemed to be for large-landowning households to underreport the extent of their landholdings, while several of the smaller landowning households (particularly those which had lost control over a portion of their land in the recent past) tended to exaggerate.

The Data Collection

The formal data collection process consisted of four sets of questionnaires:

1. Basic data questionnaires, covering mainly landholdings, other assets, and household size and composition
2. Household questionnaires on labor allocation, income, and consumption
3. Farm management questionnaires
4. Child care surveys.

The variables contained in each of the questionnaires are listed in Hart (1978: appendix A).

Assets and household size and composition. Data on landholdings proved by far the most difficult. In practice, determining how much land each household controlled turned out to be a continuing process of attempting to unravel the enormously complex system of land arrangements, and it is quite possible that the figures on land ownership, operation, and control that finally emerged do not take account of all the arrangements in which households were involved. The official documents on landholdings (the so-called "Letter C") which are used as the basis for land taxes provided the starting point. Thereafter, however, a considerable amount of detective work was necessary in order to try to determine renting, pawning, and sharecropping arrangements, as well as the accuracy of the Letter C. Much of this was an informal process, in which the two interviewers from the village visited a number of households that were directly or indirectly involved in land arrangements with households in the sample. Also, in the numerous problematic cases, the interviewers went to the fields with household members in order to get an estimate of the size of each plot and its status. It should be stressed that it was only after considerable familiarity with the sample households that much of this information emerged; even so, I suspect that several of the largest landowning households did not provide information on all their landholdings, and there are probably a number of additional intricacies of which I was not aware.

In comparison with landholdings, information on other assets was relatively easy to obtain. In the case of home gardens, we made maps, measured the area, and subtracted the area of the house in order to establish the area available for cultivation. Also, although there are various types of arrangements between tenants and owners, these appear to be far more straightforward than with rice land. Livestock were imputed for their market value, of which people seemed to be fairly certain. When asked to place a value on their houses and household possessions, there was also little hesitancy and a remarkable degree of consistency. I suspect that part of the reason is that particularly since the pest infestation there had been a great deal of selling and pawning of both agricultural and nonagricultural assets, and hence considerable interest in assessing the present market value of possessions. For example, the most common item of household furniture is a bed-frame (*amben*)—in a number of poorer households this is the only item of furniture. There was a great deal of consistency in the value placed on the *amben*, according to quality (teak, coconut wood, or bamboo) and condition. Questions relating to jewelry and gold were not asked. These involve too great an invasion of privacy, and people do not wish to divulge information on gold and jewelry for fear of theft. Thus, the data on nonagricultural assets refers to a standard set of items rather than a comprehensive inventory and probably involves relatively large underestimates, particularly in the case of wealthier households.

Information on household size and composition was adjusted continuously to take account of people who had joined or left the household. In general, adults had only a vague idea of their age, and much of this information is pure guesswork.

In the case of children born in the preceding five years, we were able to check village records, and this information is probably reliable. However, it was difficult to establish the ages of older children, and we had to keep revising these data when additional pieces of information emerged.

Labor allocation data. The final household questionnaire was based on a thirty-day recall period. The activities were all predefined, and each household member aged six and over was asked how many days in the preceding month he or she had spent in each activity and how many hours per day. Questions were also asked on returns to labor, location, and travelling time required.

The questionnaire took six months to devise. During this time, we combined a great deal of continuous observation and time budget data in order to establish both the range of activities and the period over which people seemed able to remember with a reasonable degree of facility. Several factors soon became evident. First, people appeared to have quite accurate notions of time, and questions about time devoted to various activities seemed meaningful. In part, this may be because virtually all households in the village are practicing Moslems and regularly pray five times a day at set times.

An important additional reason why the majority of Sukodono people appear to have clearly defined concepts of time has to do with the way in which work is organized. The distinction between "task-orientation," where the working day shortens or lengthens according to the task, and "timed labor" (Thompson, 1967) is apposite. Thompson's central argument is that, once wage labor becomes the dominant arrangement, concepts of time undergo important changes. Workers experience a distinction between their own time and their employer's time. The employer "must *use* the time of his labour, and see it is not wasted: not the task but the value of time when reduced to money is dominant" (ibid.: 61). Most of the time spent in income-earning activities in Sukodono is organized in the form of wage labor, in which the length of the work day for men and women is clearly defined. In addition, people tried as far as they could to arrange work contracts in advance.

These considerations bear on a second factor that soon became evident, namely, that poorer households appeared to find the recall process far easier than wealthier ones and also seemed more willing to disclose information. These differences were particularly marked for women. Poorer women who were heavily involved in wage labor as well as housework had to organize their time carefully and tended to follow a set pattern every day. Wealthier women, most of whom did not participate in income-earning activities, tended to be more task-oriented and casual; as Thompson puts it, "social intercourse and labour are intermingled." They appeared to have far more difficulty recalling how much time they spent in various tasks, and the interview process was generally more tiresome. As far as housework is concerned, we also found that, in poorer households (in which most members were usually involved in income-earning activities), tasks such as food preparation were sometimes performed by different people on different days, but that the time spent in food preparation did not vary much. In wealthier households, however, the division of labor within the household tended to be more clearly delineated, but the time spent in various tasks more variable. Differences between rich and poor households in ability and willingness to recall and divulge how they spent their time were even more marked in the gathering of income and consumption data.

Some indication of the biases suffered by the labor allocation data emerged from the child care surveys, which gathered daily time budgets for all household members in households with children under three. A comparison of the time budget with the monthly labor data revealed that certain types of low-productivity, income-earning activities on a sporadic basis tended to be underestimated. For example, we came across instances of people working at night on such tasks as tying together strands of coconut leaves for roofing, weaving different types of fishing equipment, and so forth, which were not reported in the monthly questionnaires. These types of activities were concentrated in poor households, and their work duration is underestimated accordingly. As the survey progressed, it also became evident that the work duration of fishpond owners was being overestimated.

Although the quantitative data are obviously flawed, I doubt whether more refined procedures would have altered the conclusions of this study significantly. A far greater methodological shortcoming is the imbalance between the quantitative and qualitative information. Although I devoted an enormous amount of time and effort to the former, the latter proceeded in a rather random and unsystematic fashion, partly because, as the survey progressed, I became aware that some of the most important questions were very different from those that I originally set out to answer.

VILLAGE GOVERNMENT AND ITS RELATIONS WITH THE STATE

Virtually all the villagers are orthodox Muslims, and this religious homogeneity is matched with an extraordinarily stable village government: the village headman (*lurah*) has held the position since the late 1940s. Contrary to what its religious composition might lead one to expect, the village is not uniformly supportive of the PPP (the officially sanctioned and controlled Islamic party). Instead, an important reason why the *lurah* has maintained his position through the New Order is that he is an unequivocal supporter of Golkar.

The main cleavage in the village is between the *lurah*'s family and that of the *carik* (village secretary) who adheres to the PPP. Despite the different political alignments of the dominant factions, the major struggle for power at the time of the survey was not being fought along party political lines. In anticipation of the *lurah*'s (involuntary) retirement, the two families were preparing their youngest sons as candidates; however, the *carik*'s son—a better educated and more intelligent individual than the *lurah*'s offspring—had declared himself to be an active Golkar supporter. In spite of this, his remarkably effective efforts to mobilize village support for a "self-help" health care program were brought to an abrupt halt by supravillage authorities.

The *lurah*'s compliance with Golkar in this strongly Islamic area perhaps provides part of the explanation for the comparatively high degree of autonomy that the village government is able to exercise in certain spheres of village policy. Most important is the ban on sales of land to outsiders, which is by no means a universal (or, it seems, even a common) phenomenon. The advantages that this monopoly over the land market convey to the village elite are discussed more fully below; in addition, by maintaining the comparatively closed character of the village, it has facilitated the *lurah*'s continuing control.

Although the orthodox Islamic character of the area as a whole may to some extent enhance the bargaining power of village government officials vis-à-vis supravillage authorities, the overall relationship is essentially one of clientist dependence. There are also strongly contradictory elements inherent in these relationships, nicely illustrated by two incidents. The first, discussed in considerably greater detail by Williams and Satoto (1983), concerns the efforts by Ali, the *carik*'s son and future candidate for *lurah*, to mobilize local resources for a health care program. His success in organizing and inducing the villagers to contribute both resources and labor represented a tremendous threat to the *lurah*'s authority and his son's candidacy. The extent of local organization involved in the health care program was also a source of concern to supravillage authorities right from its inception. Thus, when it became clear that Ali's efforts had succeeded beyond all expectations, the *lurah* received considerable support from the *kecamatan* authorities in subverting the program and ultimately destroying it.

The second incident illustrates how the superior power of the state apparatus can be brought into play against village government officials when interests conflict. In the dry season of 1976, the state-run sugar factory requisitioned about 30 ha of the best-irrigated rice land in the village for sugarcane cultivation. The cane was to be produced under the euphemistically termed *tebu rakyat* (people's sugarcane) system, whereby farmers whose land was included in the specified area received credit for cane cultivation but were required to cover all costs of production and sell the cane at the official (and highly uncertain) price when it was harvested. Further, they were obliged to bear the risk of crop failure. According to detailed calculations by several cultivators, even the most optimistic sugar yield and price conditions would produce far lower income than eighteen months of rice crops. In this instance, the villagers were united in their opposition to the state, and the village meetings convened to discuss the matter were unusually vociferous. The *lurah*'s efforts to use this palpable opposition in order to head off the authorities backfired; the official response was to insist that village government officials exchange equivalent areas of their salary lands with those whose land fell within the requisitioned area and that they assume responsibility for cane cultivation.

VILLAGE RESOURCES AND TECHNOLOGY

Sukodono is part of a well-established irrigation scheme, and some 60 percent of the 200 ha of *sawah* (wet-rice land) is fully irrigated. With the exception of a small area bordering on the coast, much of the rainfed *sawah* can also be double-cropped.[1] Brackish water fishponds (20 ha) and ocean fishing constitute important secondary sources of income.

According to a 1974 Agro-Economic Survey census, the total population of Sukodono was 2,149 (770 people per sq. km.). This is somewhat higher than average for Central Java, but the pressures of population on physical resources are probably less intense than in villages with the same sort of ecological base.[2] Table 8 presents data on average population densities and land use in coastal villages in the same *kabupaten* (regency). In most of these villages, brackish water fishponds and ocean fishing constitute the predominant economic activity.[3] Thus, although Sukodono is located in Kendal *kecamatan* (subdistrict), it is more comparable with the average structure of economic activity in

1. As on much of the north coast, the main irrigation problem is drainage. Terra suggests that the north coast was one of the earliest areas of wet-rice cultivation in Java (1958), but Geertz observes that "because of severe water-control problems . . . the north never became the center of a developed agrarian culture comparable to that of the interior" (1963: 45).

2. In 1971 the average for Central Java was 650 per sq. km., and for Java as a whole, 560 per sq. km.

3. For analyses of production activities in the coastal zone—particularly artisinal fisheries—see Collier et al. (1977). Brackish water fishponds in Sukodono are discussed below.

TABLE 8. Population Densities and Land Use in Coastal Villages in Kendal Regency and in Sukodono

Subdistrict	NO. OF COASTAL VILLAGES	AVERAGE VILLAGE AREA (HA)	AVERAGE POP. PER VILLAGE	AVERAGE DENSITY PER KM²	Average land use (%)				PERCENT FISHING VILLAGES
					RICE FIELDS	FISHPONDS	RESIDENTIAL/ HOME GARDENS	OTHER	
Tugu	7	509	2586	508	20	41	14	25	43
Kaliwungu	4	725	3172	438	34	44	10	12	0
Brangsong	2	351	2805	799	72	16	11	1	0
Kendal	10	162	1355	835	59	16	12	13	80
Patebon	9	305	1948	638	56	20	15	9	100
Weleri	12	194	2436	1259	78	2	14	6	92
Cepiring	12	238	2495	1049	69	7	18	6	25
Sukodono village		280	2149	768	71	7	14	8	

Source: Saropie 1975: tables 12 and 13.

Cepiring.[4] As may be seen from table 8, average densities in Cepiring—where a large sugar mill is located—exceed 1,000 people per square kilometer. The reason why population pressure in Sukodono is somewhat below the average for its ecological type is probably due largely to the nature of village government and its policy of closing the village to outsiders.

With its rich clay soil and comprehensive irrigation system, Sukodono is well suited to modern technology but vulnerable to pest infestation. From the mid-1960s, national improved rice varieties (Shinta and Bengawan) were planted extensively, and in the late 1960s the village joined the first Bimas program (see chap. 2). While the IR varieties were unpopular (due to disappointing yields and poor taste), the C4 variety was widely adopted. By the wet season of 1972–1973, more than 50 percent of the rice fields were planted with C4, and many farmers were growing three crops in thirteen to fourteen months. The fairly rapid spread of high-yielding varieties was brought to an abrupt halt by two sets of pest problems. Initially rats attacked the crops, followed in the 1973–1974 wet season by a severe infestation of brown planthoppers (*nilaparvata lugens*), which affected most of the north coast and several other areas of Java and Bali.[5] In an attempt to combat the pest infestation, farmers adopted simultaneous planting and various forms of pesticide application, including aerial spraying, were made. Most important, there was a significant reversion to local varieties, which are less vulnerable to pest attack. By the dry season of 1976 (the second half of the survey period), several large landowners had managed to obtain IR36 and other varieties that are resistant to attack by planthoppers.[6] Smaller peasants, with their more restricted access to subsidized credit and inputs, continued to plant the local varieties.[7]

4. Although Sukodono is similar to the two villages in Brangsong, the latter area has historically been less involved in sugar cultivation than Kendal, Patebon, Weleri, and Cepiring.

5. According to entomologists, poor drainage and staggered planting produce conditions in which larvae multiply rapidly. For discussions of the extent of planthopper (*wereng*) attack, see various issues of the *Bulletin of Indonesian Economic Studies*, "Survey of Recent Developments" since 1975.

6. Entomologists point out, however, that it is highly likely that new biotypes of planthoppers will develop with the capacity to attack the new varieties.

7. A number of farmers, unable to repay Bimas loans after crop losses, were not

Brackish water fishponds (*tambaks*), the other chief resource of the village, are constantly expanding through a process of siltation. Highly priced milkfish are cultivated in the ponds. In addition, the incoming tides deposit shrimp and fish in the ponds, which are harvested nightly. Despite a number of technological problems surrounding the cultivation of milkfish, the ponds were in general highly lucrative and access to them was closely associated with control over rice land.

LAND DISTRIBUTION AND TENURIAL ARRANGEMENTS

Access to land is the single most important source of power within the village. Any analysis of land distribution in Java must distinguish explicitly among landownership, land operation, and control over land (which takes account of pawning, renting, and sharecropping arrangements). Not only do these three facets of land distribution often differ widely in the same population, but each of them pertains to a different set of issues and carries different implications. Following Penny and Singarimbun (1973), landownership, operation, and control are defined as follows.

Land owned refers to the area over which a household has ownership, use, and disposal rights (*hak milik*) as defined by the 1960 Agrarian Land Law. I have also defined it to include *tanah bengkok,* which is rice land allocated to village government officials in lieu of payment. Rights to this type of land are more limited than those to fully owned land, but village government officials generally hold office for extended periods, during which time *bengkok* land is regarded as virtually equivalent to fully owned land. Land owned is an important, although partial, measure of the household's physical resource base.

---

permitted to rejoin the program despite press reports of a moratorium on Bimas debts in areas heavily affected by pests. During a brief visit I made in 1978, several informants estimated that 70 to 80 percent of the *sawah* was planted with pest-resistant modern varieties. Mention was also made of small farmers' getting access to credit and inputs from a group of larger farmers, and also of an increase in advance sales of the standing crop (known as *tebasan*). For a discussion of government actions to increase the availability of pest-resistant varieties, see "Survey of Recent Developments," *Bulletin of Indonesian Economic Studies*, 1977 and 1978.

land worked

Land operated is defined as land owned plus rented in plus sharecropped in minus rented out minus sharecropped out. Although central to an analysis of farm management and resource use, this is a misleading measure of access to land.

this is best measure of ldt based income not wealth

Land controlled is the best single measure of access to land because it represents the total area from which the household derives income. In the case of renting, land controlled is defined as the area owned plus half the area rented in minus half the area rented out; the rationale is that, if a household owns and operates land, it receives a return to both labor and land.

rental ones rent paid = 1/2 ... prod. value of land

Land rented out yields a return only to land, whereas land rented in represents a return only to labor. As far as sharecropping in and out is concerned, the area added to or subtracted from area owned is based on individual data for each household on the proportion of the crop that a sharecropping household pays to the landlord or that a household that sharecrops out land receives from the sharecropper.[8] This procedure underestimates somewhat the area controlled by households that sharecrop land from others, because the usual practice is for the sharecropper to cover all costs. The measure of rice land controlled standardizes land quality by deflating the area of inferior rainfed land by 0.7.

sharecropped essentially sre

Escrow rent x = $25/1/6 purchase ?= $250

The distribution of rice landownership, operation, and control among the eighty-six sample households in the wet season of 1975–1976 is described in table 9.[9] Although the paucity of national information on land distribution precludes any detailed comparisons, one can get a rough idea of how the distribution of land in Sukodono compares with the national averages.[10] The Gini coefficients of concentration for rice land (*sawah*) holdings calculated from the Agricultural Census data are as follows: West Java, 0.4693; Central Java, 0.4139; East Java 0.4351 (Montgomery and Sugito 1976: 40). Table 10 re-

8. The Sharecropping Act of 1960 specifies that a sharecropper who covers the costs of production should receive 50 percent of the yield; I found that sharecroppers were frequently receiving only one-third of the yield, particularly in cases where land had been pawned and was being sharecropped.

9. The Agro-Economic Survey census collected data on land owned, and this was used as the basis for stratification. Closer questioning revealed that many of these data were incorrect; this is discussed in detail in Hart (1978: appendix B).

10. The 1973 Agricultural Census excluded those with less than 0.05 hectares of rice land or 0.1 hectares of dry land.

TABLE 9. Percentage Distribution of Landownership, Land Operation, and Land Control in Sukodono

Size Groups (ha)	Ownership		Operation		Control	
	HOUSEHOLDS	LAND	HOUSEHOLDS	LAND	HOUSEHOLDS	LAND
	0 %	0 %	0 %	0 %	0 %	0 %
None	48.8%		34.9%		33.7%	
0–0.100	2.4	0.4	7.0	1.5	12.8	2.0
0.101–0.200	0	0	11.6	4.1	7.0	2.9
Subtotal	**51.2**	**0.4**	**53.5**	**5.6**	**53.5**	**4.9**
0.201–0.300	5.8	3.8	11.6	7.3	9.3	5.5
0.301–0.400	9.4	8.0	8.1	6.3	11.6	10.1
0.401–0.500	4.6	4.8	8.2	8.4	5.8	6.2
Subtotal	**19.8**	**16.6**	**27.9**	**22.0**	**26.7**	**21.8**
0.501–0.600	12.8	16.5	4.7	6.2	7.0	9.4
0.601–0.700	5.8	9.4	2.3	3.6	3.5	5.7
0.701–1.00	2.3	5.0	4.6	8.8	0	0
Subtotal	**20.9**	**30.9**	**11.6**	**18.6**	**10.5**	**15.1**
1.01+	**8.1**	**51.1**	**7.0**	**53.8**	**9.3**	**58.2**
Total	100.0	100.0	100.0	100.0	100.0	100.0

ports Gini coefficients of the distribution of *sawah* in Sukodono, using each of the three measures of landholdings discussed above, and both including and excluding those with less than 0.05 ha of *sawah*. In comparing these results with the national figures, it should be noted that, unlike the national estimates, the Gini coefficients in table 10 are calculated from ungrouped data; because grouping tends to reduce the coefficients, the Gini coefficients for Sukodono are probably somewhat closer to the national averages.

Another interesting feature of table 10 is the dramatic increase in the Gini coefficients when the landless are included. From the data discussed in chapter 3, it seems reasonable to suppose that the degree of landlessness in Sukodono is of roughly the same order of magnitude as the national average. Geertzian notions of "poverty sharing" would lead one to expect that land operated is more evenly distributed than land owned. This clearly is not the case in Sukodono, primarily because of complex tenurial arrangements, whereby large farmers gain control over the land of those in the small to medium range.

Table 11 summarizes the data from a set of micro studies conducted in the early to mid-1970s that provide information on rice land distribution in villages where rice cultivation is the predominant economic activity, all of them in central Java. Although the number of observations is clearly too small to provide a basis for generalization, it would appear that Sukodono is roughly in the middle range in terms of the proportion of households that does not own any rice land.

TABLE 10. Gini Coefficients for Rice Landholdings in
           Sukodono

Rice Land	*Excluding landless households*	*Including landless households*
Owned	0.4627 (N = 44)	0.7251 (N = 86)
Operated	0.5851 (N = 57)	0.7250 (N = 86)
Controlled	0.5891 (N = 57)	0.7277 (N = 86)

TABLE 11. Comparative Data on Rice Landownership in Central Javanese Villages

STUDY	VILLAGE	REGENCY (AREA OF CENTRAL JAVA)	DENSITY (POPULATION/ SQ. KM)	Percentage of households owning			AVERAGE SIZE OF RICE HOLDING (HA)
				RICE FIELDS	HOUSE PLOT ONLY	NO CULTIVABLE LAND	
Utami & Ihalauw (1973)	Nganjat		1958	44%	16%	40%	0.37
	Kahuman	Klaten (South)	1962	44%	22%	34%	0.59
	Pluneng		1835	31%	26%	43%	0.62
Penny & Singarimbun (1973)	Srihardjo	Bantul (South)	1290	63%	15%	22%	0.30
White (1976)	Kali Loro	Kulon Progo (South)	750	63%	27%	10%	0.23
Franke (1973)	Lestari	Pemalang (N. Coast)	n.a.	36%	25%	39%	n.a.
	Sukodono	Kendal (N. Coast)	768	51%	32%	17%	0.79

Two of these studies (Penny and Singarimbun 1973; White 1976a) analyze the relationship between the ownership and control of rice land.[11] Their conclusions accord with the findings of this study in that the proportion of households that controls no rice land is smaller than the proportion that does not own any rice land (in Srihardjo and Kali Loro, the proportion of households that does not control any rice land is 6 percent and 21 percent, respectively). The opportunities for a landless household in Sukodono to gain access to land are, however, limited and determined primarily by kinship relations. The majority of landless households that operate land are the children of landowners who sharecrop from their parents or other close kin. The "near-landless" are generally defined as those controlling less than 0.2 ha of irrigated rice land, the area that several researchers have estimated as being the minimum needed by a household of five in order to meet its staple food needs (White 1976a; Franke 1973). In Sukodono, this group of households constitutes nearly 55 percent of the total; comparative figures for Srihardjo and Kali Loro are 67 and 74 percent, respectively.

At the other end of the distributional spectrum, those with more than 1 ha constitute 8 percent of households and own 51 percent of the rice land, while 9 percent of such households control 58 percent. By far the most economically powerful group in the village, these households fall into two broad categories: those who are members of the village government and who control *bengkok* land in addition to their own (frequently quite substantial) holdings; and a small group of households owning brackish water fishponds. The privileges inherent in political office are evident from the fact that *bengkok* land in the village comprises 32.5 ha (over 16 percent of the village *sawah*) allocated among fourteen village government officials; *bengkok* holdings range in size from 9.4 ha (the headman) and 4.6 ha (the secretary) to 0.975 ha (the irrigation officials). Further, *bengkok* land is usually the most fertile and best irrigated (Utami and Ihalauw 1973).[12] The average area of rice land controlled

11. The definition of control over land used by Penny and Singarimbun is similar to that I used. White's definition is slightly different, in that he regards land rented in as fully controlled.

12. Both Utami and Ihalauw (1973) and White (1976a) comment that village government officials are, on the average, by far the most economically powerful group.

by fishpond owners is 1.24 ha, compared with 0.6 ha for the sample as a whole, and control over rice land tends to be an important prerequisite for access to fishponds.[13]

This small group of large land controllers is actively engaged in land relationships with other classes. Six of the eight households in this group were involved in either renting in or renting out of land, or both. Renting in is used as a means of consolidating landholdings, whereas more fragmented (and possibly less fertile) plots tend to be rented out. On balance, two-thirds of the households controlling more than one hectare are net renters-in of land; in total, they rent out 2.77 ha and rent in 5.77 ha. In contrast, nine small landowning households (those in the 0.2–0.5 ha range) rent out a total of 2.50 ha.

The control that large landowners exert over the land of small to medium landowning households extends far beyond relatively straightforward rental arrangements. Eleven households in the ownership range of more than 0.3 but less than 0.6 ha (40 percent of this group) were, at the time of the survey, sharecropping on their own land after having received a lump sum "rental" from one of a small group of large landowners in the village.[14] These "sharecroppers" cover all the costs of production and hand over two-thirds to three-fifths of the yield—usually the former. These arrangements (known as *disewakan-sakap lagi* or renting out and sharecropping back) in effect reflect the operation of an active credit market; the "rent" payment is a loan that is repaid by sharecropping. The amount of the loan is inversely proportional to the period of the contract, which ranged from three to twenty-five *oyod* (planting seasons), and averaged nine.

From the viewpoint of the lender, these arrangements are extremely lucrative; at the average yields and prices prevailing at the time of the survey, lenders were earning average returns

White also found that more than one-half the rice land was owned by 6 percent of households, most of them those of village government officials.

13. The fishponds are in a continual process of accretion as a result of soil being washed down from the hills. Obtaining use and ownership rights involves a lengthy and expensive process of negotiation with government officials.

14. One of these (a village government official) is included in the sample. As far as I was able to establish, there are four other large landowning households in the village involved in this system. I suspect that the actual number is larger than this.

in the vicinity of 150 percent per planting season (about 300 percent per year). There is, of course, a substantial degree of lender's risk inherent in these arrangements, because yields may decline in unfavorable weather and sharecroppers may undersupply labor and inputs. Lenders' efforts to minimize part of the risk explain some of the apparent peculiarities in labor market operation. The spread of these arrangements is indicative of a process of loss of control over land by the small and middle peasantry, and their increasing reliance on off-farm income. At the same time, *disewakan-sakap lagi* is one of the few sources of large-scale credit available to small landowners, and the alternative would probably be outright sale.

ASSET CLASSES: CRITERIA AND CHARACTERISTICS

This section uses the information on land distribution to divide households into three categories or "asset classes" on the basis of their control over rice land and fishponds. There are two major objections to this procedure. First, a unidimensional measure like landownership is narrow and may produce a distorted picture of patterns of control over resources. Although this argument applies in a number of rural settings, it is not relevant in the case of Sukodono and probably in much of lowland Java because control over land is closely correlated with access to other resources.

The second and more basic objection is that agrarian class structure cannot be understood simply in terms of the distribution of resources, but must take account of relations among people. This argument is clearly valid and informs the analysis of agrarian differentiation in this book. The key point is that the purpose of dividing the sample into asset classes is to provide a framework within which the evidence on inter- and intrahousehold relations and patterns of resource allocation can be examined more closely. As such, it constitutes a point of departure for the analysis of agrarian class formation rather than a priori specification of rural class divisions.

The criteria for defining asset classes are based on the degree of control over primary productive assets (rice land and fishponds) that a household must have in order to meet its staple food needs, and attain self-sufficiency. Real income in rural Java is most usefully measured in kilograms of milled rice equivalents. The widely accepted level of real income necessary to meet "basic needs" in rural Java is 240 kg. of milled rice equivalent per person per year (Sajogyo 1974b; Penny and Singarimbun 1973). This corresponds to the concept of *cukupan*, which Penny and Singarimbun define as follows: "The Javanese peasantry, both its rich and its poor, have long had a concept of what constitutes 'enough.' The word they use is *cukupan*. It is applied to what they see as being the reasonable needs of the ordinary peasantry" (1973: 20). One-half of this "poverty line" level of income is estimated as sufficient to cover rice needs in a rice-based diet, and the remaining 120 kg. of milled rice equivalent is allocated to nonrice food and nonfood items.

It is important to note that this is an average *per person* estimate, based on the assumption that a household of five needs a minimum income of 1,200 kg. of milled rice equivalent per year in order to achieve a satisfactory standard of living, and it is, therefore, averaged over different age and sex groups. For my purposes, it is more useful to convert the *cukupan* level of income to a consumer unit basis in order to correct for interhousehold differences in household size and composition. The coefficients used for standardizing to an "adult male equivalent" are a slight adaptation of those applied by Epstein (1962):[15]

	Age	*Coefficient*
Children	1	0.10
Children	1–3	0.30
Children	4–5	0.50
Children	6–9	0.65
Females	10–15	0.75
Males	10–15	0.80
Females	16+	0.80
Males	16+	1.00

15. Epstein (1962) uses the Lusk Coefficients, which were developed specifically in the context of a low-income rural environment, by the Indian government's "Report on an Enquiry into the Conditions of Agricultural Workers in the Village Archikarahalli, Mysore State."

The average number of people per household in the sample is 5.17; applying these coefficients, there are an average of 3.87 "adult male equivalent" consumer units per household. Thus, the minimum level of real income per consumer unit is approximately 300 kg. of milled rice equivalent per annum, of which 150 kg. represents rice needs. It is interesting to note that Scott cites French geographers in Indochina whose estimates of the minimal number of kilograms of rice equivalents needed by an adult male is also approximately 300 (1976: 16).

The criteria I have used in specifying an operational definition of the three main groups of households in the village are based on the relationship between minimum needs and control over production assets, and are as follows:

Class I: Households that are self-sufficient in the sense that they can attain a net income of at least 300 kg. milled rice equivalent per consumer per unit per year from their own productive assets.

Class II: Households that control sufficient productive assets to cover staple food needs (150 kg. of rice per consumer unit) but not enough to achieve a minimum subsistence level of income.

Class III: Households that do not control sufficient productive assets to meet even staple food needs.

Data from a farm management survey of rice production in the wet season 1975–1976 provide the basic information on yields and costs. There is a marked inverse relationship between farm size and yields per hectare, which is quite a common feature of production patterns in a low-income rural environment. On the basis of these data on average yields by farm size group and costs of production,[16] and using the official conversion rate from wet paddy into milled rice, a household of five members (four consumer units) must control at least 0.575 ha of rice land producing two crops per year in order to attain a net income of 300 kg. per consumer unit per year from its own land. Thus, Class I households are defined as those that control at least 0.14 ha of rice land per consumer unit. Also included in Class I are a few households that control less rice

16. These costs include hired labor and mate value of work by household members.

land than this minimum, but that own and operate at least 2 ha of fishponds.

Given the inverse relationship between farm size and yields per hectare and the lower proportion of purchased inputs on small farms, the amount of land that a household must control in order to meet its rice needs is somewhat less than half of that required for full self-sufficiency. My estimate of 0.24 ha per household (600 square meters per consumer unit) as the lower cut-off point for Class II is slightly above the minimum of 0.2 ha estimated by White (1976a) and Franke (1973).

Applying these criteria, the asset class breakdown of the eighty-six sample households in the wet season (ninety-two in the dry season) is:

	Wet season	*Dry season*
Class I	20 (23.3%)	23 (25.0%)
Class II	29 (33.7%)	29 (31.5%)
Class III	37 (43.0%)	40 (43.5%)

Table 12 describes average ownership, operation, and control of *sawah* in each of the three asset classes. The two households in Class I that do not own any *sawah* are both large fishpond owners who had sold *sawah* to purchase fishponds. In total there are ten households in Class I that own and operate fishponds (an average of 2.5 ha) and the average size of rice holdings of these households is relatively large.[17]

The distribution of secondary productive assets—primarily home gardens and livestock—is somewhat more equitable than that of rice land but is clearly closely related to control over rice land (table 13). A household that does not own the land on which its house is sited is known as a *penumpang*. Although a *penumpang* household does not generally pay rent, the landowner is entitled to the produce of any trees on the land surrounding the house. On the whole, *pekarangans* (home gardens) in Sukodono are smaller and less intensively cultivated than has

17. Several other Class I households hold options to purchase fishponds, which, at the time of the survey, were not ready for operation. There is also one Class II household involved in fishpond sharecropping, which is unusual in Sukodono.

Use of F statistic?

- assumes that variance w/in each "class" is equal
(How can you argue that?)

- what conclusion can you draw?

- supposed to relate to reject Ho that X̄ equal across groups
- but here we don't get df. or prob.

Sukodono

12. Interclass Differences in Ownership, Operation, and Control of Rice Land in Sukodono

	Class I N = 20	Class II N = 29	Class III N = 37	F Statistic
Rice landownership				
No. of owners	18	23	3	
Percent of owners	90.0	79.3	8.1	
Average area, owners only (ha)	1.321	0.451	0.331	6.38
Average area, all households (ha)	1.189	0.357	0.027	23.44
Rice land operation				
No. of operators	19	29	9	
Percent of operators	95.0	100	24.3	
Average area, operators only (ha)	1.415	0.311	0.158	8.92
Average area, all households (ha)	1.344	0.311	0.038	18.05
Rice land control				
No. of controllers	19	29	9	
Percent of controllers	95.0	100	24.3	
Average area, controllers only (ha)	1.355	0.305	0.088	11.84
Average area, all households (ha)	1.287	0.305	0.021	23.52

been reported elsewhere in Java (Stoler 1978), although fruit trees grow in abundance.

Three of the largest Class I households own water buffalo, which are used for ploughing and harrowing of their own land, and are also hired out. According to several informants, the buffalo population of the village has declined over time, and there has been a marked substitution of human for animal labor in land preparation. Eleven households own ducks, and for three of these (two in Class II and one in Class III) the sale of duck eggs constitutes an important source of income. Virtually

TABLE 13. Interclass Differences in Ownership of
Secondary Productive Assets and Household
Possessions in Sukodono

	Class I	Class II	Class III	F Statistic
Home garden and house plot ownership				
No. of owners	18	28	22	
Percent of owners	90.0	96.6	59.5	
Average area, owners only (m²)	1060	488	384	
Average area, all households (m²)	954	471	228	8.31
Home garden availability for cultivation[a]				
No. of operators	18	28	22	
Percent of operators	90.0	96.0	59.5	
Average area, operators only (m²)	881	387	313	4.19
Average area, all households (m²)	793	373	186	6.33
Average value of other productive assets (Rp'000)[b]				
Livestock	60.1	8.8	2.1	4.99
Agricultural equipment	14.8	7.0	3.0	5.02
Fishing equipment	1.4	1.6	1.1	0.18
Average value of household possessions (Rp'000)				
Kitchen equipment	28.9	8.1	4.4	20.15
Furniture	65.3	18.3	5.3	26.96
Durables[c]	30.9	2.3	1.3	25.08
Vehicles	34.2	2.2	0	2.74
Average value of house (Rp'000)	504.0	161.2	29.1	33.57

[a]The total area of the compound minus the area of the house.
[b]Rp 420 = U.S. $1.
[c]Sewing machines, radios, tape recorders, and clocks.

all households own a few chickens, which are an important form of saving for the poor because chickens are frequently sold in the slack season before the harvest.

Although the quality of housing and the range of household possessions of even the wealthiest households are modest by Western standards, interclass differences in "household capital" are enormous (table 13). Apart from the mosque and school, there are no brick buildings in the village. Better-quality houses are constructed of wood and have tiled or cement floors and shingled roofs, but the typical landless household lives in a small windowless hut made of woven bamboo with mud floors, containing little other than a wooden bed frame. Indeed, one can often guess quite accurately how much land a household controls from the size and quality of its house and furnishings.

DEMOGRAPHIC STRUCTURES, KINSHIP, AND EDUCATION

An interesting question is whether the household's internal structure is systematically related to its control over resources. For instance, it is possible that the landless and small landowning groups contain a high proportion of young households with close kinship relations with those in the larger landowning groups. Such relations may shape the household's long-term prospects for upward mobility as well as its short-term access to income-generating opportunities, and could mean that age (or the household's phase in its life-cycle) is a more useful criterion for distinguishing among households.

Table 14 provides the basis for examining the relationship between demographic structures and control over resources. Anthropological studies have shown that, although the nuclear household is the modal organizational form in rural Java, there is a wide range of more complex arrangements (Geertz 1961; White 1976a). This is indeed the case in Sukodono; 73 percent of the sample households are nuclear, but the remaining 27 percent comprise several other organizational forms, which, to some extent, are related to control over resources. The primary examples are extended households and female-headed households, which are concentrated in Classes I and III, respec-

TABLE 14. Demographic Characteristics of Asset Classes in
Sukodono

	Class I	Class II	Class III
Distribution of households among household types and developmental stages[a]			
Nuclear and Related:			
Early	20	24.1	27.0
Early-mid	20	17.2	8.1
Mid	15	34.5	35.1
Mid-late	20	10.3	2.7
Late	10	3.4	10.8
Extended	15	6.9	—
Female Head	—	3.4	16.2
Total	100	100	100
Household size			
Max. no. of people[b]	5.65	5.69	5.05
Average no. of people[c]	4.98	5.64	4.90
Average no. of consumer units[d]	3.91	4.21	3.59
Average age of head of household	44	41	40
Distribution of people among age/sex groups			
Children 0–5	12.4	17.1	16.0
Females 6–9	6.4	6.4	5.2
Males 6–9	6.4	8.3	9.6
Females 10–15	6.2	9.3	7.7
Males 10–15	10.6	10.1	10.2
Females 16+	27.9	23.5	30.3
Males 16+	30.1	25.5	21.2
Total	100	100	100

[a]See footnote 19 for definitions.
[b]Maximum no. of people per household during 12-month period.
[c]Average no. of people per household per month.
[d]See text.

tively.[18] All other households have been categorized into one of five life-cycle phases, and a particularly striking feature of table 14 is the broad similarity across asset classes in the proportion of households in each developmental stage.[19]

Within Class I, the eight largest landowners (those who control more than 1 ha) share two important demographic characteristics: with a single exception, they are older and contain a far smaller proportion of young children than other households in Class I or in the village as a whole. This is not, however, a reflection of a Chayanovian process, whereby a high ratio of workers to consumers has facilitated the acquisition of additional land. Five of these households contain five or more members, but virtually all children over the age of six are in school. Two are households that have already broken up, the offspring having either left the village or been given land. Half of the remaining twelve households in Class I are young couples with a relatively large number of children under the age of ten who have inherited land from wealthy parents. Members of this group have comparatively high levels of education, and their chances for upward mobility lie in strong social, political, and economic connections with other privileged households and with those outside the village. These two groups, which together comprise about 15 percent of village households and 70 percent of those in Class I, are the true "village elite" in terms of their position in the village hierarchy and their links with the outside world. The remaining 30 percent of Class I consists of relatively large (average, seven members) households that would lose some of their economic advantage if they were to split up and that do not exert nearly the same degree of influence on village affairs.

18. Two other household forms are also related to asset status. Several of the wealthiest households in Class I had "adopted" a boy between the ages of 10 and 16 to take care of water buffalo; these children are generally from poor, unrelated households and are provided with board, lodging, and a nominal allowance. The other fairly common non-nuclear form—a parent of the husband or wife living in the household—is limited to classes II and III. Other types of non-nuclear households (those containing widowers and nonrelated adults) are unusual.

19. The criteria for grouping households into development stages are as follows: Early—all children below the age of 6; Early-mid—at least one child over the age of 10; Mid—most children in early teens; Mid-late—at least one child aged 15 or more; Late—elderly couples (usually childless or with no children at home).

The most characteristic feature of Class II households, as mentioned earlier, is that the vast majority of them (about 83 percent) are linked with other households through tenurial relations. In most cases (eighteen of these twenty-four households), this is a consequence of the household having fallen into debt and either rented out land or entered into one of the complex sharecropping arrangements described earlier. These households are spread over various life-cycle phases, and household size and composition does not seem to be systematically related to loss of control over land. It is interesting to note, however, that the five Class II households that are not involved in tenurial relations with other households are all in the mid or mid-late phase of their life-cycles, which suggests that a low dependency ratio may be a necessary condition for avoiding loss of control over land, but that it is not a sufficient one.

There are twelve households (six each in Classes II and III) that share important similarities. They comprise a group of young households that own no land but operate small plots by virtue of kinship relations. Six of them are sharecroppers on land owned by close relatives (generally parents), and another six rent in tiny pieces of land, three of whom had inherited the resources that enabled them to do so. This is a reflection of an interesting practice in Sukodono. Rather than a small plot of land being subdivided among heirs, the tendency is to sell the land and distribute the proceeds or, in the case of somewhat better-off households, for one heir (usually the oldest son) to pay off the other siblings. The six households of this type that have been grouped in Class III qualify for inclusion in terms of inability to meet even staple food needs from their own resources, but in terms of kinship and other relations most of them are probably closer to Class II. If these six households are excluded from Class III, the proportion of landless households in the early stages of expansion falls from 27 to 13 percent, and the average number of young children per Class III household also declines.

If those with some access to land and high dependency ratios constitute a relatively privileged group among Class III households, the most destitute are two clearly identifiable groups, which have the lowest dependency ratios and smallest average household size, namely, female-headed households and elderly couples with few or no children. A few of the women in the former group are widows, but for the most part they are divorced. The remaining Class III households are those that are slightly better off by virtue of their internal structure, but that have far fewer links with powerful groups than demographically similar households in Class II.

The comparatively high proportion of female-headed households and childless elderly couples in Class III is the main reason for the small average household size in this group (table 14). Another important difference among asset classes is that variations in household size over the course of the year were greatest among those in Class I; in table 14 this is indicated by the difference between the maximum and average number of people in the household. The reasons derive in part from the higher proportion of extended households in Class I; those who comprise the "secondary" portion of the household tend often to be more mobile. Also, several Class I households have children attending school elsewhere in Java who only return to the village during vacations.

The data on average and maximum household size also reflect the low levels of migration during the period of the survey. Although many people engage in wage labor outside the village, few actually left the village.[20] Extensive inquiries about past migration revealed an interesting pattern. Among wealthier households, it seems that primarily younger, relatively well-educated males have tended to leave the village.[21] In the poorest households, however, many of those who have left are women seeking jobs as domestic servants, although many probably fall into prostitution (Papanek 1975). During the period of the survey, the only rural-urban migration that I was able to document involved about seven young women from poor households (one of them in the sample) going to Jakarta in the slack period of the wet season; most, though not all, returned.

20. The single exception to this among households in the sample was a man from a landless household who left the village during the slack period of the wet season. His brother helped arrange a job for him in a village about 50 km. from Sukodono.

21. The predominance of relatively young, well-educated migrants is consistent with national patterns; see Aklilu and Harris (1980).

TABLE 15. Interclass Differences in Educational Levels in Sukodono

| | Years of formal education | | | | | |
| | FEMALES | | | MALES | | |
Age Group	Class I	Class II	Class III	Class I	Class II	Class III
7–9	2.4	1.4	1.0	1.5	1.4	0.8
10–12	2.3	1.4	1.4	3.0	(3.7)[a]	2.5
13–15	5.0	1.7	1.6	2.3	(4.5)[a]	3.0
16–20	4.2	1.8	1.1	2.4	(3.4)[a]	3.2
21–30	3.0	2.7	0.9	3.9	3.3	2.1
31–40	0.3	0.5	0.1	3.0	2.6	1.6
41–50	0.3	0.3	0.0	1.0	2.0	1.6
51+	0.0	0.0	0.0	2.0	0.0	0.0

[a]Figures in parentheses are years of education for nuclear household members only (see text).

The extremely low levels of education are shown in table 15. These data must be treated with caution because the number of observations in each cell (particularly in the lower age groups) is rather small. Also, these data refer only to formal schooling and do not include education acquired in religious schools (*madrasah*). There are, however, some fairly clear patterns. Among adults, particularly those over thirty, average levels of education are low, and differences between men and women are greater than those among classes. In the case of children, however, there are some marked differences between Class I vis-à-vis Classes II and III, particularly for girls. But it must be borne in mind that boys in Class I households are more than likely to attend *madrasah,* which carries high status in this strongly Islamic community.

Low and sporadic school attendance reflects the important role that children play in the domestic economy of poor households; this, together with the direct costs of education, prevents the majority of children from acquiring more than two or three years of schooling. It is likely, however, that part of the reason why the majority of households do not invest in education for their children is that the probability of obtaining lucrative employment is perceived as being quite limited. Several of the wealthiest households are, in contrast, preparing their children for government jobs, and a few have been successful.

5
SOURCES AND PATTERNS
OF LIVELIHOOD

The activities in which the men, women, and children of Sukodono engage in their efforts to earn a livelihood form the
focus of this chapter. Its purpose is to convey a picture of the
wide variations among households in sources and levels of income as well as in patterns of market involvement. In particular, the disparities in control over productive assets discussed in
the previous chapter are associated with marked differences in
access to income activities and modes of labor deployment.

INCOME-EARNING ACTIVITIES AND
LABOR ARRANGEMENTS

Wage labor was by far the most important means by which the
people of Sukodono earned a livelihood. Over the period of the
survey, more than 50 percent of the time that the villagers devoted to earning income was sold to others. Work applied to
self-owned assets—*sawah,* fishponds, and, to a lesser extent,
home gardens and livestock—accounted for less than 30 percent of directly productive labor time; the remaining 20 percent or so went to various forms of nonagricultural self-
employment, primarily fishing, gathering, and trading.

Most wage work involved heavy physical labor, but there
were important variations among and within different labor
markets in terms of the division of labor by sex, the seasonality
of work opportunities and wages, and institutional arrangements for the recruitment and control of labor. The relative
importance of different wage labor markets over the course of
the survey year is depicted in table 16.

TABLE 16. Percentage Distribution of Wage Labor Markets for Women and Men in Sukodono

	Rice inside village	Rice outside village	Sugar-cane	Fish-pond	Tobacco	Other	Total wage labor
Women	49.2	16.0	32.8	—	—	2.0	100
Men	28.1	11.4	13.0	32.5	7.1	8.2	100

The importance of rice employment cannot be understood simply in terms of the proportion of labor that it absorbs, however, because the entire economic life of Sukodono revolves primarily around the rice cycle. Patterns of seasonality and of labor input across farms exert an important influence on labor market structure as a whole, and nonrice activities often reflect adjustments to the variations in demand for rice field labor.

The Organization of Rice Production

The division of labor in preharvest rice activities is clearly stratified according to sex; seedbed preparation and care, land preparation (plowing, hoeing, and harrowing), and the removal of seedlings from the nurseries are all done by men, as are miscellaneous tasks, such as water control, fertilizing, and pesticide application. Transplanting and weeding, however, are regarded as women's tasks. All age and sex groups participate in the rice harvest, although women predominate. Women's wage rates are lower than those of men and subject to wider seasonal variations.

The reversion to local rice varieties meant that most farmers were planting more or less simultaneously, giving rise to intense seasonal fluctuations of hired labor in rice production over the year. Within the peak periods of rice cultivation (November to January and May to July in the wet and dry seasons, respectively), there was some intermonthly variation in the intensity of demand for female over male labor. The slack periods for both sexes coincided in February–March and August–September, although labor demand was on the average somewhat higher in the dry season slack period. The reason is that a group of large farmers managed to obtain pest-resistant high-yielding rice varieties harvested in September and started land preparation for the next crop by October.[1]

Patterns of labor use in the wet season rice cycle are shown in table 17.[2] The data refer to manual labor input and indicate that the absolute amount of family labor devoted to rice production differs little across asset classes.[3] The relative intensity of family labor input, in contrast, declines sharply as control over assets increases; total labor input per hectare is also inversely related to asset status, although to a lesser degree. As one would expect, the three asset classes differ most in their use of hired labor on both an absolute and a per hectare basis, with Class I households accounting for 82 percent of total hired labor compared with 16.5 percent and 1.5 percent in classes II and III, respectively. The predominance of large landowners on the demand side of the village rice labor market is even more marked: the six Class I households that cultivate more than 1 ha comprise 10 percent of the rice-cultivating households but employ more than 60 percent of the total hired labor.

A disaggregated analysis of hiring behavior also provides insights into a question that has long puzzled analysts of farm management data: Why do small peasants frequently hire labor? Part of the answer may lie in the fact that some "small operators" control other productive assets, in which case the household enterprise could be quite large. For instance, there are two Class I households contained in the two smallest farm size groups; both are fishpond owners for whom rice cultiva-

1. Rainfall in the dry season of 1976 was exceptionally low, and yields were below normal. The demand for harvesting labor was, therefore, lower than in the wet season.

2. These data were collected in a farm management survey at the end of the wet season rice cycle from the 57 households in the wet season sample of 86 that cultivated *sawah*, plus 3 of the 6 households in the expanded dry season sample of 92. Farm management data were also collected at the end of the dry season. The labor input data show similar patterns, but yields were affected by the dry conditions described in chap. 4; the incidence of crop damage was fairly evenly spread across farm size groups.

3. Class I households spend more time in pure supervision. The line between supervisory and manual labor is sometimes a narrow one, and family members nominally engaged in "manual labor" along with hired workers generally devote most of their attention to supervision.

TABLE 17. Preharvest Labor Use in Rice Production in
Sukodono: Wet Season Rice Cycle

	Average Hours[a]			F Statistic
	CLASS I	CLASS II	CLASS III	
Absolute labor input				
Family labor				
Female	42	80	38	1.1
Male	88	122	78	1.0
Total	130	202	116	2.1
Hired labor				
Female	479	82	22 *583*	4.4
Male	510	61	18 *589*	3.9
Total	989	143	40	4.2
Total absolute labor input	1119	345	156	3.7
Total input per hectare				
Family labor				
Female	64	349	299	1.8
Male	123	447	741	7.8
Total	187	776	1040	6.5
Hired labor				
Female	358	268	190	2.0
Male	328	179	153	3.2
Total	686	447	343	2.8
Total labor input per hectare	873	1243	1383	2.1
No. of observations:	21	29	9	

[a]A female labor day (transplanting and weeding) is between four and five hours, whereas the average male labor day is seven hours; see Hart (1978: appendix A). In contrast to the data in table 18, these data exclude supervisory work and travelling time. They also exclude such activities as protecting the crop from birds in the period before the harvest and preparing food for laborers. The labor input data are broken down by activity in Hart (1978; table B-11, appendix B). Hours of labor equivalents on the basis of a conversion ratio are used by the village people. It is said that a team of two water buffalo and two men working for four hours is equivalent to 2.5 seven-hour male labor days of hoeing. Wage rate differentials reflect these differences precisely.

tion is merely a sideline activity, and both hire labor. Second, the average figures on hired labor may mask considerable variation in labor use and work arrangements. Of the eight Class III households in the smallest farm size group, three did not hire any labor at all. The bulk of labor hiring is accounted for by the only female-headed household with access to land. Lacking male family labor and unable to afford to hire in labor on a regular basis, this woman contracted out part of the operation of her 0.1 ha plot to a small landowning household in return for half of the crop. If this household is excluded, the average amount of labor hired by Class III households in the smallest farm size group falls to 17 hours.

Probably the major reason why small farmers hire in labor is to perform the tightly time-constrained operations, in particular transplanting. Transplanting requires on the average 35 days of labor per hectare, a figure that varies very little across farm size groups. In order to finish transplanting in a day, even the smallest farm households would need to hire in labor unless they contain at least two female members of working age. Excluding the household mentioned above, over 60 percent of the labor hired by Class III households was for transplanting; most of the remainder was for plowing and harrowing.

Among the large village employers, recruitment and supervision of labor also vary according to the time constraint of the operation and the availability of labor. For instance, at the peak of the transplanting season most labor recruitment and organization was contracted out to a small group of women, and relations between workers and employers were largely indirect and impersonal. A somewhat similar situation obtained in the case of male activities that fell in periods of heavy labor demand; at these times, the large landowners tended to delegate recruitment and some supervision to *buruh dekat* (literally, "close laborers").[4] In periods when jobs were scarce, however, the system of access to these jobs was far more complex.

---

4. The relationship that a *buruh dekat* has with his patron is usually of long standing. Many of them were brought into the landowner's household as children in order to care for water buffalo. When they reached adulthood, the landowner often arranged and paid for the wedding, and provided the *buruh dekat* with a small piece of land to sharecrop, extended loans at little or no interest, and provided assistance in times of illness, etc. In return, the *buruh dekat* was expected to be at the beck and call of the landowner, and perform a variety of unpaid tasks. When not needed, the *buruh dekat*

One element of this system (discussed more fully in chapter 7) is that in intravillage labor markets workers do not openly request employment; rather they must be "invited." Whether or not a laborer received an "invitation" to work and the terms on which he or she was invited depended largely on the nature of other connections with the employer. Although harvesting was even more tightly time-constrained than transplanting, the system of access to harvesting opportunities and the share that the harvester received were more analogous to slack period activities in that they were contingent on the larger network of relations between owner and harvester.

Nonrice Wage Labor

The two main forms of nonrice wage labor—fishpond and sugarcane work—represent opposite extremes in terms of recruitment, supervision, and worker-employer relations. Although fishpond labor is comparatively arduous, it also offered workers a considerable degree of security and the status of *buruh tambak* (fishpond laborers) was at least as high as that of those who only engaged in rice labor. Sugarcane work, in contrast, was considered highly demeaning. The relative stability of fishpond labor is reflected in wage rates, which tended to be 10 to 15 percent lower than those for peak season rice labor; however, they were substantially above the prevailing slack season wage received by sugarcane laborers.

Fishpond labor is exclusively male, and seasonal variations in labor demand are comparatively small. Most of the work consists of shovelling silt from the ponds; some shovelling must be done regularly to prevent accumulation, but the amount of labor can be varied. In consequence, labor use in fishponds tended to move counterseasonally with that in rice production. Another important characteristic of fishpond labor is that the owners are seldom present at the ponds during the day and therefore exercise little direct supervision.

---

was permitted to work for others. However, these types of relationships are limited; even the largest landowner retained no more than two *buruh dekat*. As far as I could establish, kinship ties were unusual in these arrangements.

Fishpond laborers fall into two categories: those who are hired on a permanent basis; and those who are hired to do additional shovelling work. Most of the permanent laborers are landless, whereas many in the second group are from the class of small landowners. Several fishpond owners also cultivate large areas of rice land, and at peak periods of rice labor demand sometimes divert permanent fishpond laborers to rice field work.

Particularly for women and children, sugarcane work constituted an important source of employment in slack periods of rice production. Most of these jobs were outside the village, often at a considerable distance, although in the dry season sugarcane was cultivated within the village. An analogous form of employment was *tebasan* rice harvesting. This arrangement entails the sale of a standing crop to a *penebas* (broker) who hires a team of harvesters, often although not always from another village. Most of this work was also outside the village.[5]

In general, worker-employer relations in sugarcane labor and rice-harvesting work outside the village tended to be far more impersonal and commercialized than those in fishpond labor or rice work within the village. A good indication of this is that prospective sugarcane or *tebasan* workers are not invited but must seek work. Particularly when work opportunities are scarce, those who already have a relationship (*hubungan*) with a sugarcane supervisor (*mandur*) or rice-harvesting broker (*penebas*) are more likely to obtain work, but such a relationship offers none of the certainty of employment that seasonal fishpond workers have. The most obvious factor in these

5. At the time of the survey, there were three *penebas* (brokers) operating in Sukodono and several more in adjacent villages. None was a member of the dominant elite; rather they belonged to a small group of households who, in terms of the landholding criteria used in this study, fall in the lower ranks of Class I. They obtained credit from the privately owned rice mill in the adjacent village and contracted to sell the rice to the mill. In periods when they were inundated with requests for work, they used a method of rationing employment opportunities—either distributing cards or numbered hats. As a rule, they tended to prefer groups of household members working together, because the various operations involved in the harvesting process—cutting, threshing and bagging the rice, and carrying it to the roadside—can be performed more rapidly and efficiently when there is a division of labor. The *mandurs* are employees of the government-operated sugar mills. The total labor costs for cultivating a given area of sugarcane are prespecified, and thereafter the *mandurs* have a free hand in terms of wage determination and recruitment.

differences is location; most of the sugarcane and *tebasan* labor is outside the village. However, the key difference between the two sets of labor markets is that *penebas* and *mandurs* exercise constant direct supervision over their workers, whereas modes of labor control in most intravillage labor arrangements are usually far more subtle and indirect.

Nonagricultural Self-Employment

Fishing is the most important form of nonagricultural self-employment for males. There were no full-time fishermen in Sukodono, and fishing boats were not used. Rather, all fishing was conducted on an individual basis, using equipment that varied from elaborate bamboo scissor-like contraptions with lanterns on the end to simple nets.[6] The period during which it is possible to make a living from fishing without boats is only about four to six weeks. Even then, the returns to fishing are highly variable; a man may spend all night fishing and earn anything between the equivalent of about four days' wage labor and virtually nothing.

The female counterpart of fishing was gathering edible plants, snails, frogs, and fuel from the village and its environs. In general, such food and fuel were used for home consumption; among poorer households, however, the sale of these commodities formed a secondary source of income. In periods when no wage labor was available, several women and children devoted virtually all of their working time to this activity, known locally as *bangsang*. The returns to gathering were without exception lower than wage labor.

The market structure in the area was such that trade and handicrafts were far less prevalent than has been observed in other Javanese villages (Stoler 1977b). Only a small group of women was involved in trading. In general, trading involved buying groceries from the local town and selling them in the village or selling village produce (primarily eggs, coconuts, and bananas) in the local town. In both cases, the price differential was in the vicinity of 15 to 20 percent. There were also a few

6. During the peak fishing season (usually around January), men fish through the night and sell the catch early in the morning at the neighboring village fish market.

large rice traders who operated outside the village. Trading was primarily a female activity, although some of the wealthiest and most influential men in the village acted as brokers (*makelaars*) in large-scale transactions in the village and its environs.

Although almost all households engaged in repairing roofs, sewing, making brooms, and a multitude of similar activities, few did so on a commercial basis. Indeed, this comparatively low level of small-scale nonagricultural self-employment seems to be a distinguishing feature of Sukodono. Other village studies in Java have revealed extensive involvement in such activities as coconut sugar production, bamboo weaving, pot and brick making, and the preparation and sale of small quantities of cooked food (White 1979). These activities tend to be characterized by low capital requirements, some degree of flexibility in terms of timing, and generally low returns to labor. In periods of limited wage labor opportunities, they may constitute a primary source of income, whereas in peak employment periods they are either abandoned or performed in the late afternoon or evening when workers have returned from wage jobs.

The availability of sugarcane work seems to be the main reason why the level of nonagricultural self-employment was so low in Sukodono, although the methods of data collection do tend to underestimate these types of activities (discussed in chapter 4). Ocean fishing and fishpond labor also expanded the available set of income-earning activities, but the fishing season was brief and fishpond labor was concentrated among a few comparatively privileged men. In contrast, low-wage sugarcane labor was generally available to even the poorest women and children.

LABOR ALLOCATION ACCORDING
TO CLASS, SEX, AND AGE

The household-level labor allocation data presented in table 18 have been deflated by the number of "worker units" (people over the age of 10) in order to correct for interclass differences in household size. Several patterns emerge. First is the consistently inverse relationship between asset status and work duration, with a landless person spending on the average 27 percent

TABLE 18. Household Patterns of Labor Allocation in Sukodono

| | Average annual hours and percentages per "worker unit"[a] | | |
	CLASS I	CLASS II	CLASS III
Own production			
Rice	308.6 (16.3%)	183.6 (9.1%)	23.7 (1.1%)
Fishponds	579.4 (30.6%)	28.3 (1.4%)	—
Home garden	14.8 (.78%)	20.2 (1.0%)	2.4 (0.1%)
Livestock	32.1 (1.7%)	66.6 (3.3%)	56.1 (2.6%)
Other[b]	113.5 (6.0%)	133.2 (6.6%)	10.7 (0.5%)
Subtotal own production	1048.4 (55.4%)	431.9 (21.4%)	92.9 (4.3%)
Wage labor	151.9 (8.0%)	770.9 (38.2%)	1289.0 (59.7%)
Trading	169.6 (9.0%)	123.1 (6.1%)	73.7 (3.4%)
Fishing & gathering	26.0 (1.4%)	252.7 (12.5%)	314.6 (14.6%)
Subtotal income-earning activities[c]	1395.9 (73.7%)	1578.6 (78.3%)	1770.2 (82.0%)
Housework[d]	497.5 (26.3%)	437.4 (21.7%)	389.7 (18.0%)
Total work	1893.4 (100%)	2016.0 (100%)	2159.9 (100%)

[a]Persons aged 10 and over.
[b]Tobacco and dry land crops.
[c]Including time spent travelling to and from work.
[d]Excluding child care.

more hours in income-generating activities than a member of a large landowning household.[7] In the case of housework, however, the pattern is reversed. There are also marked differences among classes in the types of income-earning activities. As may be seen from table 18, a huge proportion of the labor time of Class I households is concentrated in work with productive assets owned by the household (frequently the supervision of hired laborers) and in trading. Landless households, by contrast, are primarily involved in heavy manual wage labor, while the small-landholding group occupies an intermediate position.

The methodology of data collection not only underestimates the work duration of the landless but also overstates that in the large-landowning class. Table 18 shows that the bulk of "own production" work in Class I is concentrated in fishponds. The reason for these long hours is that some fishpond owners frequently spend all night at the ponds supervising the lucrative nightly shrimp catch, which is sold at a nearby fishmarket early in the morning. Although owners sleep in huts at the ponds, all the time spent there was counted as working time. If the ten fishpond-owning households are excluded, the average amount of time that Class I households devote to own production is reduced considerably, because interclass differences in time spent in rice production are considerably smaller than farm size differences.[8]

The direct relationship between time devoted to housework and asset status assumes additional significance when one takes account of variations in household technology. As was shown in table 13, the value of kitchen equipment owned by Class I households is significantly higher than that of classes II and III. In preparing food, Class I households use up to three stoves simultaneously, whereas those in Class III seldom use more than one. Also, both the type of stoves and the cooking utensils

7. Even though the data collection methods underestimate the work duration of poorer groups and overstate the work duration of Class I fishpond owners, the inverse relationship between asset class and work duration is statistically significant; for F-statistics estimated from the monthly data, see Hart (1978: appendix B).

8. The data on family labor use in rice production in table 17 are rather different from those in table 18, because the former refer to manual labor, whereas the latter include supervision, time spent preparing food for laborers, and bird-scaring activities.

used by Class I households are generally more efficient than those used in poorer households. The main reason why Class I women spend substantially more time in food preparation is that wealthier households consume more elaborately prepared meals more frequently than poorer ones. Class I households are also more involved in *selametans* (ritual feasts), the preparation of which requires huge amounts of work. Hired laborers are occasionally given cooked food in lieu of part of their cash wages; however, time spent preparing this food has been included in "own production."

A second major source of interclass disparities in housework derives from patterns of shopping. Class I households generally shop in the local town where most food prices are 10 to 15 percent lower and the range of goods available is more extensive than in the village; wealthier women often spend nearly the whole morning shopping once or twice a week. Landless households, in contrast, purchase food on a daily basis from nearby village shops. Shopping is usually done in the late afternoon, when income earners have returned from work, and takes no more than a few minutes. All households sweep and clean everyday, but there is a strong positive relationship between asset status and house size, number of rooms, and the amount of furniture (table 13). In general, therefore, goods and time tend not to be substitutable. On the contrary, increases in household capital are accompanied by a rise in the amount of time spent in housework, and this additional time probably contributes substantially to household welfare.

Women perform the bulk of housework, and there is little interclass variation in the proportionate allocation of housework between females and males.[9] There are, however, substantial differences among asset groups in the division of directly productive labor by sex, with the proportion of income-earning work undertaken by women increasing sharply as the household's asset base decreases. This is partly attributable to the consistent interclass differences in the ratio of females to males (discussed in chapter 4). Table 19 corrects for these disparities

9. The proportion of housework performed by females in each class is as follows: Class I, 91.9 percent; Class II, 90.9 percent; and Class III, 93.6 percent. See Hart (1978): table V-3, p. 128.

TABLE 19. The Proportionate Allocation of Income-Earning Activities Between Females and Males in Sukodono

	Class I	*Class II*	*Class III*
Females			
1) Percent of household income-earning work performed by females	20.7	32.6	43.7
2) Females as a percent of household members aged 10 or older	45.1	47.9	54.9
1 : 2	0.46	0.68	0.80
Males			
1) Percent of household income-earning work performed by males	79.3	67.4	56.3
2) Males as a percent of household members aged 10 or older	54.9	52.1	45.1
1 : 2	1.44	1.29	1.25

in demographic structure by computing the ratios for females and males between the percentage of total household income-earning time performed by females and males, respectively, and each sex group as a percentage of total household members over the age of 10. These ratios show that, even when one takes account of the fact that landless women and girls comprise a larger percentage of the population than in the other two classes, the proportion of income-earning work that they undertake is comparatively large. Conversely, the share of males in income-earning work relative to their proportion in the household population is directly related to asset status.

Moving to the individual level, one of the most striking features is the heavy involvement of girls from the landless class in income-earning activities, particularly wage labor (fig. 1 and table 20).[10] A comparison of these figures with those for adult women in Class III suggests that a female child born into a landless household is destined from an early age to a work pattern that changes very little over the course of her life cycle.[11]

For women too, more assets are accompanied by less time spent in income-earning activities and by shifts in the types of activities in which women are engaged (fig. 2 and table 20). Landless women spend nearly 80 percent of their directly productive time in heavy physical labor, often far from home in slack periods of rice production. Wage labor by women from small-landowning households is mainly on rice fields within the village, and they tend to withdraw from wage labor in periods when rice labor availability in the village is low. Class I women seldom participate in wage labor; their involvement in off-farm work is largely confined to trading, by far the most lucrative income-earning activity in Sukodono. Of course the returns to trading represent in part a return to capital; however a household's land base is important in determining access to capital and hence to trading opportunities.

The pattern for males is different. Figure 4 shows that, though there are massive interclass differences in terms of the proportionate allocation among activities, total hours spent in income-earning activities by the average adult man differs little among asset classes. However, the Class I data are heavily inflated by fishpond owners; if they were excluded, the average work duration of large-landholding men would drop substantially. The general inverse relationship between assets and total working time is clearly evident among boys in the 10 to 15 age group (fig. 3). Much of the "own production" work performed by boys is care of livestock, and in the case of Class I households includes working time of boys "adopted" by the household to herd water buffalo. In comparison with girls, boys from landless households spend a relatively small proportion of their

10. Separate monthly data can be found in Hart (1978: appendix B, tables B-1 to B-6).

11. Both the survey and general inquiries revealed that it is not unusual for poorer women to return to income earning quite soon after childbirth, particularly if there are children in the 6 to 9 year old age group in the household. White (1976a) reports similar patterns.

TABLE 20. The Allocation of Labor by Individuals According to Sex, Age, and Class Status in Sukodono (Average hours per year)

Sex and age group	Class	Own production	Trading	Wage labor	Fishing & gathering	Total income-earning activities[a]	Housework[b]
Girls	I	43.7	0	54.2	23.6	121.5	361.9
10–15	II	43.8	42.8	416.8	173.8	677.2	437.6
	III	17.5	5.4	1168.2	190.3	1381.4	390.8
Women	I	243.7	368.3	158.6	28.4	799.0	1215.8
16+	II	179.9	327.2	640.1	105.4	1252.6	1002.5
	III	40.8	1323.4	1201.5	160.9	1535.6	801.8
Boys	I	508.8	0	51.9	53.6	614.3	29.8
10–15	II	432.4	45.5	302.2	486.1	1266.2	57.0
	III	176.8	14.4	553.7	583.4	1328.3	36.8
Men	I	2245.9	108.4	209.6	13.9	2577.8	90.0
16+	II	837.5	1.0	1288.5	308.5	2435.5	81.3
	III	139.3	56.2	1877.1	410.3	2482.9	60.2

[a]Including travelling time.
[b]Excluding time spent in child care.

Own production
Trading
Wage labor
Gathering
Housework

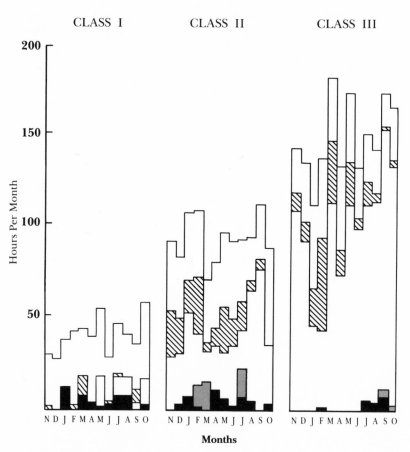

FIGURE 1. Average Labor Hours, Females, 10 to 15, Sukodono

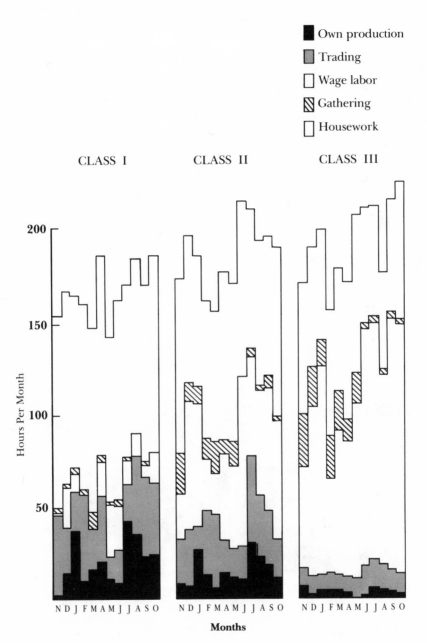

FIGURE 2. Average Labor Hours, Females, 16 and Over, Sukodono

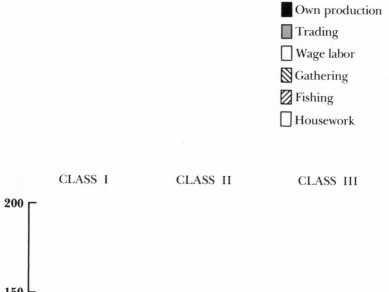

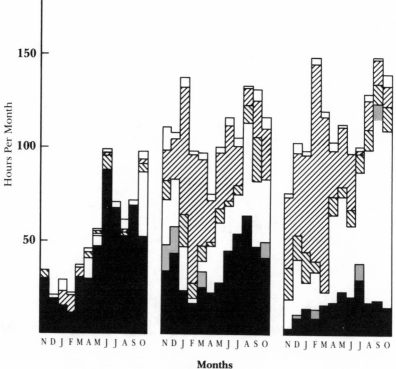

FIGURE 3. Average Labor Hours, Males, 10 to 15, Sukodono

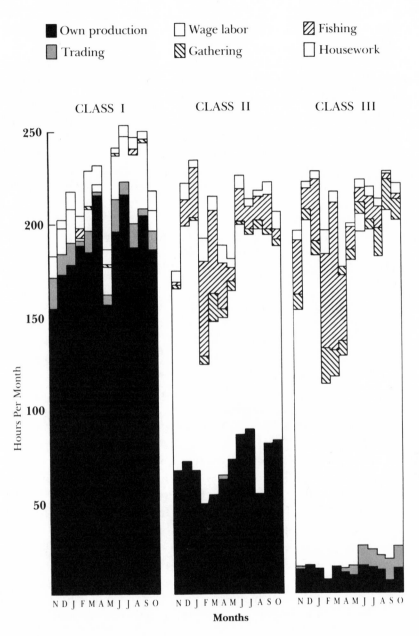

FIGURE 4. Average Labor Hours, Males, 16 and Over, Sukodono

time in wage labor due to important differences in the nature of female and male labor markets.

The limited involvement of boys in the 10 to 15 year age group from Class I households in income-earning activities is directly related to patterns of school attendance (Hart 1978: table B-9, appendix B). In addition to the relatively high opportunity costs of school attendance by older children (particularly girls) in the landless class, income levels are such that school fees and the costs of books and stationery—particularly for secondary school—represent a heavy burden to poor households.

There is a less direct but important relationship between the role of children in the 6 to 9 age group in the domestic economy and school attendance. Some young boys from poorer households spend substantial amounts of time cutting grass for animals, collecting fuel, fetching water, and so forth, but the proportion of children engaging in these activities is rather small.[12]

Although children's participation in directly productive work is limited, they are heavily involved in the care of younger siblings. Detailed time budgets of households with children under the age of 3 revealed substantial amounts of time—ranging between 10 and 12 hours a day—devoted to the care of infants and young children.[13] The child care survey showed that virtually all children from the age of 5 or 6 are involved in looking after younger siblings. There are, however, important differences between households in which the mother participated in income-earning activities and those in which she was at home most of the time. In the latter case, children frequently looked after the baby while the mother was busy with household tasks or out shopping; as a rule, this was in the early morning or in the afternoon when they returned from school. Among poor households, however, children usually took care of younger siblings while mothers were at work during the day. This pattern clearly has important implications not only for the low school

12. For detailed information on the income-earning activities of children in this age group, see Hart (1978: table B-8, appendix B).

13. However, child care is frequently combined with housework; see Hart (1978) for more detailed information.

attendance, but also for the marked intermonthly variations in school attendance rates. The headmaster of the local school complained about sporadic school attendance and attributed much of it to children being needed at home to take care of younger siblings when both parents were at work.

This evidence is consistent with White's arguments that, even though children's direct contribution to income is small until about the age of 10, they play a vital role in releasing adults from routine tasks within the household (1976a). The importance of children's activities in the domestic economy is inversely related to the household's physical resource endowments. These considerations are facets of two more general points, namely, the greater need for intrahousehold coordination in poor households and important differences among asset classes in modes of adjustment to seasonal changes in wages, prices, and job availability.

PATTERNS OF MARKET INVOLVEMENT

In terms both of levels and monthly variations in consumption and income, small-landowning households are far more similar to the landless than to the large-landowning group. Over the year, the average level of consumption per consumer unit in kg. of milled rice equivalents per consumer unit for each of the three classes was:

Class I 590
Class II 335
Class III 274

Although the discrepancy between the average level of consumption in Class II and III households is relatively small, it is significant in view of the "poverty line" of 300 kg. of milled rice equivalent per consumer unit (chapter 4). The typical landless household achieved the minimally acceptable level of consumption in only two of the twelve months, whereas the small landowners on the average seldom fell below it.

The most significant differences among asset classes lie in the sources from which they derive consumption and the associated patterns of market involvement (table 21). Small-landowning households were able to cover a substantial proportion of consumption from their own produce, whereas the landless relied on the market for most of their consumption needs. These divergences are even more striking if one considers only rice, by far the most important food item for all Sukodono households. The insecurity inherent in Class III households' dependence on market-purchased foodgrains is intensified by large fluctuations in the retail price of rice, which moved inversely with wages and job availability. Despite these price fluctuations, the typical landless person maintained a virtually constant level of consumption across months. Furthermore, the average of 12.5 kg. per month is identical with the minimum defined by the poverty line and amounts to approximately 1,450 calories per adult male equivalent consumer unit per day.

To understand how the poorest households coped with inverse price and wage movements, we need to look more closely at income patterns. Figure 5 depicts monthly net income flows from own production, trading, and manual labor (which includes wage labor, fishing, and gathering) but excludes rents, sales of assets, gifts, and other sources of income. The relatively small intermonthly income fluctuations in landless households are in part a reflection of the deployment of additional female and child labor in periods when wages declined. The other important way in which many poor households attempted to deal with insecurity was to restrict consumption. Although the typical landless household managed to achieve an annual income of 300 kg. of milled rice equivalent per consumer unit, the average consumption was about 10 percent lower.

The probability that this discrepancy between income and consumption formed part of a strategy of insurance rather than accumulation is suggested by evidence contained in table 22, which shows nonlabor sources of income. These data refer to February and March, the *paceklik* (scarcity season) before the main wet season harvest, which was the period of greatest stress. Table 22 illustrates several important points. First, as far as I could establish, there appears to be little short-term consumption borrowing in Sukodono. The extent to which such

TABLE 21. Consumption Patterns in Sukodono (in percentages)

	Class I	Class II	Class III
Sources of Total Consumption			
Own produce	30.4	29.9	4.1
Expenditure	62.5	52.2	71.6
Wage labor	1.3	6.7	14.5
Trading stocks	1.8	3.4	1.8
Fishing & gathering	0.5	0.5	4.5
Gifts & festivals	3.5	3.5	3.5
Allocation of Consumption			
Rice	34.8	58.0	61.4
Nonrice food	22.8	19.7	21.2
Nonfood	42.4	22.3	17.4
Sources of Rice Consumption			
Own produce	80.7	56.2	7.1
Purchased	18.6	37.4	75.6
Harvest share	0.7	6.4	17.3

borrowing did take place was primarily in the form of rice to be repaid after the harvest. Among Class III households, it was generally those with wealthier relatives who obtained such loans. The majority of landless households who encountered deficits had only two options: selling possessions or pawning them in the government pawnshop in the local town. Sales generally involved poultry, small livestock, and, occasionally, implements such as hoes. In a desperate situation, a household might dismantle and sell part of its house. More often, however, they resorted to pawning anything from kitchen utensils to gold and jewelry. People were of course reluctant to disclose information about gold transactions. I suspect, however, that even quite poor households acquired minute amounts of gold as insurance against sudden increases in rice prices and/or shrinking employment opportunities.

There is an active capital market in Sukodono; it operates primarily via the renting/sharecropping arrangements de-

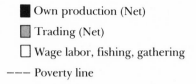

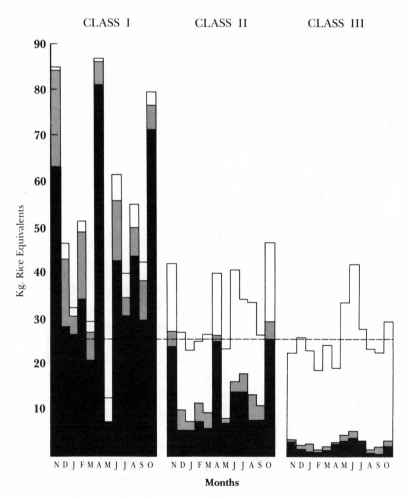

FIGURE 5. Income by Source in Rice Equivalents per Consumer Unit in Sukodono (Excluding periodic income)

TABLE 22. Borrowing, Pawning, Renting, and Sales of
Assets in the Preharvest Scarcity Period in
Sukodono (February and March)

	Class I	Class II	Class III
Borrowing[a]			
Percent of households	—	10%	30%
Average amount (rp)	—	7000	2527
Pawning			
Percent of households	—	24%	35%
Average amount (rp)	—	4343	1238
Sales of chickens, goats,			
and implements			
Percent of households	—	41%	57%
Average amount (rp)	—	1596	1283
Sales of gold, jewelry, and bicycles			
Percent of households	10%	10%	—
Average amount (rp)	21750	21000	—
Land: rent receipts			
Percent of households	5%	7%	—
Average amount (rp)	150000	11000	—
Land: renting/sharecropping			
Percent of households	—	3%	—
Average amount (rp)	—	25000	—

[a]Mainly rice.

scribed in chapter 4. Given the high returns from these arrangements, it is possible that the large landowners of Sukodono do not consider petty money lending worthwhile. The chief consequence is that only those who own land have access to credit on any meaningful scale. Only one Class II household entered into such an arrangement in February–March; however a number had previously contracted these types of debts, and during the course of the year several more did so for the first time or extended existing contracts. Access to credit is connected in important ways with the structure of access to employment.

In general, there seems to be a U-shaped relationship between asset status and the extent of market involvement. For instance, table 21 showed that the proportions of consumption that classes I and III obtain from the market are substantially higher than in the typical Class II household. A similar pattern holds with respect to income from basic sources; classes I and III each derive more than 80 percent of basic income from commercial sources, whereas it is much closer to 60 percent in the typical Class II household. The high level of market involvement by the landless is driven by compulsion and is qualitatively different from that of the large-landowning group. Conversely, the degree of withdrawal from commodity markets that small landowners are able to achieve is a reflection of their somewhat more secure position relative to the landless.

6

COPING WITH SEASONALITY: STRATEGIES OF LABOR DEPLOYMENT

The way in which different households in Sukodono coped with seasonality sheds considerable light on their allocative strategies. By and large, the activity patterns of Class I households did not change substantially across seasons; although many wealthier households were engaged in a diversified portfolio of activities to which they devoted varying amounts of time, they did not evince major occupational shifts over the course of the year. In contrast, the large group of households whose livelihoods were contingent on off-farm labor income were profoundly affected by seasonality. As work availability and wages shifted across seasons, the majority of small-landowning and landless households engaged in constantly changing combinations of activities in their efforts to secure a livelihood. Even more revealing are the differences among these households.

SEASONAL FLUCTUATIONS IN EMPLOYMENT AND WAGE RATES

In order to understand how different types of households responded to seasonal variations in work availability and wage rates, we need first to examine the relationship between wage rates and the volume of employment in different labor markets. This information is contained in figures 6 and 7 for women and men, respectively. The first important point to note is that labor markets for men are far more diversified than those for

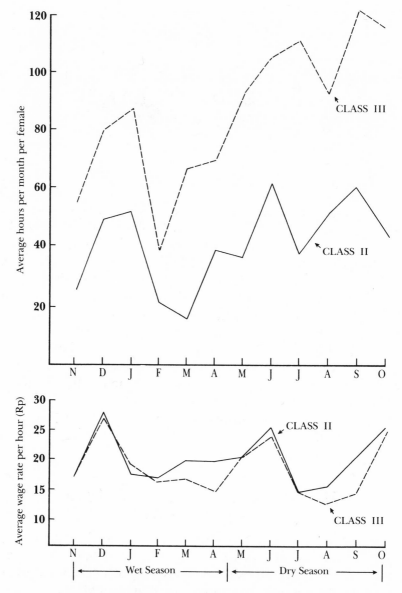

FIGURE 6. Differences Between Small-Landowning (Class II) and Landless (Class III) Females in Wage Labor Hours and Wage Rates, Sukodono

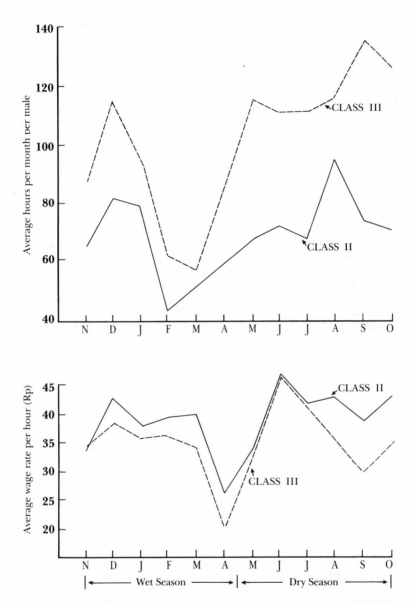

FIGURE 7. Differences Between Small-Landowning (Class II) and Landless (Class III) Males in Wage Labor Hours and Wage Rates, Sukodono

women. The lesser diversification of female labor markets is accompanied by apparently greater "competitiveness," reflected in relatively low interlabor market wage rate differentials and in a general tendency for wage rates and the volume of employment to move concurrently. In July and August, however, there were interesting interactions between the sugarcane and rice labor markets that ran counter to this pattern. Figure 6 shows that sugarcane employment in June was not particularly high, but the wage rate was the same as that in rice in order to bid women workers away from transplanting rice; thereafter sugarcane wages followed the decline in rice wages despite the substantial increase in sugarcane work, most of which was undertaken by women and girls from landless households. (Another important feature of female labor markets to be examined below is the emergence of marked differentials in returns within the rice labor market in harvesting periods.)

In addition to a wider range of wage labor markets, men had the option of self-employment in fishing. Fishing opportunities also varied seasonally, and in 1976 the peak fishing period coincided with the slack period of rice production. Figures 3 and 4 in chapter 5 showed the large increases in time spent fishing by both men and boys in classes II and III in February and March. As mentioned earlier, returns to ocean fishing were highly variable; while somewhat related to skill and equipment, there was a large risk element involved in fishing. In February and March, some men spent up to ten hours a night fishing, and the value of the catch varied between Rp 3000 or more to virtually nothing; on the average, however, returns to fishing were greater than those in wage labor.

Although the differentials among male labor markets were smaller than variations in returns to fishing, they were considerably wider than in the case of female labor markets. In particular, male wage rates were less closely linked to the demand for labor in rice production than those for women.[1] Fishpond

1. The extremely low wage rates in April, the main harvest month, are somewhat misleading. Payment for harvesting is on a piece rate basis, and the price of rice is at its lowest in this period. However, in general only the poorest men participate in harvesting; they receive much the same returns as women.

labor is a particular case in point. As with female sugarcane labor, male employment in fishponds varied countercyclically with rice; in contrast, wage rates for fishpond laborers were relatively constant and generally higher than those in other wage labor markets in slack periods of village rice production. Access to fishpond labor in slack periods of rice production was limited to a select group of households. Also, job rationing in the fishpond labor market is only one manifestation of a far more general phenomenon that is in part responsible for the interclass wage differentials depicted in figures 8 and 9.

In the case of women and girls, small interlabor market wage differentials are accompanied by relatively small interclass wage differentials, except in harvesting periods (April and September). The major difference between classes lies in the degree of involvement in wage labor, particularly in slack periods of rice cultivation. With the exception of February, landless women and girls maintained long working hours in slack months; women from small-landowning households tended to withdraw from wage labor in periods when wage rates were low.

Coincident with a more complex labor market structure, male wage differentials tend to narrow in peak periods of rice labor demand and to widen in slack periods of rice production, although the gap is smaller in the wet season slack (February-March) than in the dry season slack (August to October).[2] The reason lies partly in the availability of fishing opportunities in February and March, which is reflected in a sharp reduction of wage labor hours by men of both classes. By the slack period of the dry season, fishing was far less lucrative. Landless men increased their working hours despite sharp declines in wages; there is generally a direct relationship between wage rates and hours worked by Class II men. In this period, the wages that landless men earned were on the average 30 percent lower than those of small landowners.

2. The level of demand for rice labor in August and September was greater than that in February and March, but far lower in October than April. This more even profile of labor demand is primarily a reflection of the shift to high-yielding varieties with shorter growing cycles and the unusually dry weather. The rice harvest began earlier and was smaller than usual, but by October some of the larger farmers had commenced land preparation. A peculiar feature of the dry season slack period was the heavy demand for labor generated by government-imposed sugarcane cultivation.

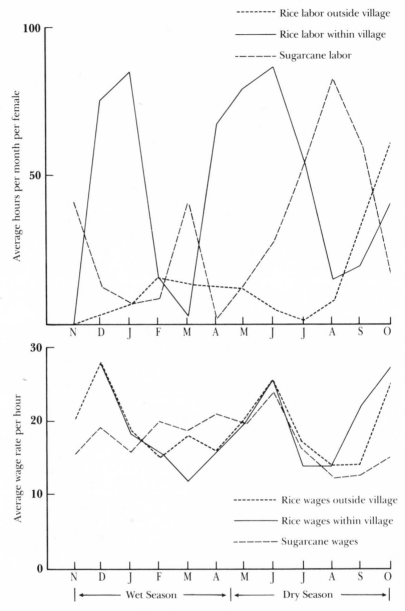

FIGURE 8. Female Employment and Wage Rates in Different Labor Markets, Sukodono

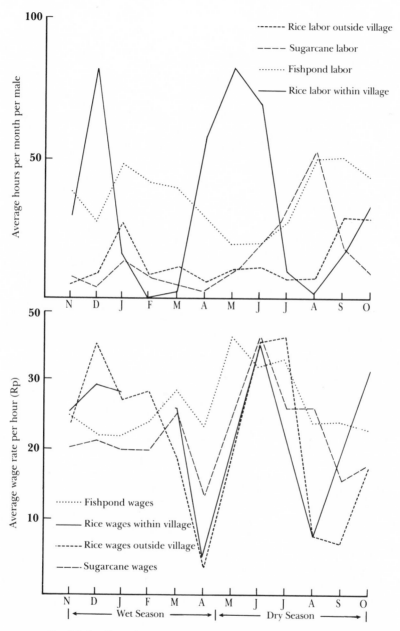

FIGURE 9. Male Employment and Wage Rates in Different Labor Markets, Sukodono

How statistically significant are these wage differentials? In order to address this question, I have estimated the following earnings function separately for males and females in each month:

$$\ln Y_{ih} = A_i + \alpha_i \ln \text{hours}_{ih} + \beta_i \ln \text{assets}_h + \lambda_{ih}(C/N)_{ih} + e_i,$$

where i refers to males and females, h to households; Y is female (male) wage labor income per household per month; "assets" is the value of productive assets controlled by the household in thousands of rupiah, and C/N is the ratio of wage labor participants in the 10 to 15 year age group to total wage labor participants in the household.

The double-log form of the model allows one to test whether the relationship between wage labor income and hours worked is linear in logarithms, which is equivalent to the proposition that wage rates are independent of hours worked. Consequently, the null hypothesis is that α is unity. In the tables, the test statistics for the hypothesis that α is different from 1 are presented in square brackets. With the "assets" variable, the null hypothesis that we are testing is that β is 0, namely, that the income males and females earn from a given number of hours of work does not depend on their asset status. Alternatively, this coefficient enables us to test the extent to which the positive association between asset status and wage rates is statistically significant. The variable representing the ratio of child to adult participants (C/N) takes account of the fact that children, particularly girls in the 10 to 15 age group, are heavily involved in wage labor in poorer households. Especially insofar as males are concerned, the wage rates earned by boys are below those of adults.

The null hypotheses with respect to α and β are, in effect, statements of standard notions of labor market competitiveness. First, from the viewpoint of the individual worker, the wage rate should be given and independent of the time that he or she spends working. Second, in the context of markets for unskilled labor where education, on-the-job training, and other skill-related factors do not influence hiring decisions and wage rates, all workers should have equal chances of obtaining a job at the prevailing wage rate.

Tables 23 and 24 report the earnings functions estimates for females and males, respectively. The results confirm that, on the whole, female labor markets are more competitive than those for male labor, although table 23 shows that there are certain periods in which the α and β coefficients for females are significantly different from 1 and 0, respectively. In five of the twelve months, women who worked longer hours had to accept substantially lower wage rates than those whose involvement in wage labor was more limited. An interesting feature is that the α coefficients diverge most from unity in periods when the demand for female rice labor in the village is at its height—transplanting and harvesting. As was explained earlier, transplanting is a heavily time-constrained operation offering wages approximately twice those for weeding and nonrice labor; the low α coefficients for December and June show that women who wished to work beyond the transplanting period had to accept lower wage rates in labor markets outside the village.

The two harvesting months in which the α coefficients are lowest (April and September) exhibit comparatively high and significant β coefficients. These findings are consistent with those of Stoler, whose study of harvesting in Kali Loro village in south-central Java reveals that landless women worked longer hours and received lower shares than those from landowning households (1977a). Within the landholding group, Stoler also found a direct relationship between control over assets and harvest shares. The main difference between Sukodono and Kali Loro in harvesting practices is the participation of males. According to Stoler, all harvesting in Kali Loro is done by women, while in Sukodono poorer men also participate in the main wet season harvest within the village and receive returns to labor similar to those of women. As one would expect, the β coefficient for males is large and significant in April.

A strong positive association between male wage rates and asset status is also evident in other months. Consistent with the descriptive evidence that asset status is linked with access to relatively high wage jobs in periods when opportunities within the village are limited, the β coefficients and their associated t-statistics are generally highest in slack periods of rice produc-

TABLE 23. Wage Labor Earnings Functions, Females in Sukodono
(Dependent variable: ln wage labor income)

Phase of rice cycle	Constant	α (ln hours)	β (ln assets)	λ C_i/N_i	R²	N
Wet Season						
Nov. Slack	2.95	0.91 [1.64] (17.6)	0.06 (2.84)	−0.13 (1.04)	0.93	30
Dec. Transplanting	3.84	0.89 [2.73] (20.9)	0.01 (0.87)	−0.02 (0.13)	0.91	61
Jan. Weeding	3.11	0.98 [0.31] (18.6)	−0.03 (1.62)	−0.20 (1.27)	0.89	58
Feb. Slack	2.85	0.98 [0.58] (32.2)	0.002 (0.02)	0.20 (1.99)	0.97	36
March Slack	2.00	1.15 [4.48] (33.7)	0.04 (1.95)	0.07 (0.59)	0.98	30
April Harvest (major)	3.22	0.86 [2.29] (15.4)	0.05 (2.29)	−0.17 (1.02)	0.79	67

Dry season						
May	Harvest/transplanting	2.92	1.00	0.03	−0.48	0.90	79
		(24.9)	[0.23]	(1.70)	(3.38)		
June	Transplanting/weeding	3.98	0.85	0.04	0.18	0.94	63
		(28.9)	[5.19]	(0.37)	(1.79)		
July	Weeding	2.80	0.99	−0.01	0.09	0.94	57
		(24.9)	[0.27]	(1.06)	(0.92)		
Aug.	Slack	2.52	0.99	0.03	−0.10	0.93	55
		(24.5)	[0.18]	(2.46)	(1.13)		
Sept.	Harvest (minor)	3.46	0.82	0.05	−0.12	0.86	61
		(18.3)	[4.17]	(2.26)	(0.76)		
Oct.	Harvest (mainly outside village)	3.67	0.91	0.11	−0.27	0.89	63
		(20.4)	[2.04]	(0.78)	(3.10)		

Note: t-ratios in parentheses. The t-ratios in brackets test whether the α coefficients are different from 1.

TABLE 24. Wage Labor Earnings Functions, Males in Sukodono
(Dependent variable: ln wage labor income)

	Phase of rice cycle	Constant	α (ln hours)	β (ln assets)	λ C_m/N_m	R^2	N
Wet season							
Nov.	Land prep.	3.48	1.01 [0.31] (31.4)	0.01 (0.63)	−0.68 (6.12)	0.95	57
Dec.	Land prep.	3.57	0.99 [0.20] (23.0)	0.04 (2.13)	−0.39 (2.69)	0.90	62
Jan.	Slack	3.40	1.02 [0.32] (13.2)	0.01 (0.60)	−0.14 (0.42)	0.78	50
Feb.	Slack	3.96	0.91 [1.45] (14.6)	0.02 (0.81)	0.20 (0.78)	0.86	39
Mar.	Slack	2.76	1.13 [2.43] (20.0)	0.05 (2.47)	−0.76 (4.25)	0.93	42
April	Harvest	2.72	1.01 [0.17] (12.4)	0.08 (2.60)	−0.51 (2.73)	0.71	62

Dry season

May	Land prep.	3.29	1.04	0.01	−0.56	0.85	63
			(17.7) [0.73]	(0.57)	(3.94)		
June	Land prep.	3.49	1.04	0.03	−0.39	0.86	61
			(17.7) [0.69]	(1.78)	(2.90)		
July	Slack	3.02	1.08	0.06	−0.67	0.89	60
			(14.7) [1.17]	(2.87)	(4.57)		
Aug.	Slack	2.78	1.11	0.07	−0.56	0.82	60
			(15.2) [1.52]	(2.89)	(2.91)		
Sept.	Harvest (minor)	2.59	1.12	0.08	−0.91	0.84	61
			(17.5) [1.87]	(3.93)	(5.29)		
Oct.	Harvest/ land prep.	3.22	1.05	0.05	−0.54	0.88	59
			(19.9) [0.94]	(2.71)	(5.37)		

Note: t-ratios in parentheses. The t-ratios in brackets test whether the α coefficients are different from 1.

tion. The exception to this general pattern is February when heavy rains precluded much wage labor, and fishing opportunities were available. In peak periods of demand for male labor other than December, the narrowing of interclass wage differentials is reflected in the low and insignificant β coefficients. Another interesting and important feature of the earnings functions for males is that none of the α coefficients is significantly less than 1; indeed in March there is a positive relationship between wage rates and hours worked. This result suggests that, unlike women, men did not have to trade off longer duration jobs against higher wage rates.

The patterns of wage disparities revealed by the earnings functions are the outward manifestation of a complex set of forces that structure and differentiate the opportunities to which different households have access.

MODES OF ADAPTATION TO SEASONALITY

Establishing the connections among the activities of men, women, and children requires a highly disaggregate analysis; I shall accordingly focus on two key months: March and October. February to March, the *paceklik* (scarcity period) before the major wet season harvest, was traditionally a time of great stress for poor households with high rice prices, low wage rates, and limited wage labor opportunities in the village. The situation at the time of the survey was exacerbated by heavy rains in February, which reduced wage labor availability for women, although by March low-wage, sugarcane labor was available at a considerable distance from the village. October was distinguished by a medium level of demand for both male and female rice labor in the village, and the October labor market structure is broadly indicative of the situation likely to obtain with a shift to high-yielding rice varieties and staggered planting.

Tables 25 and 26 summarize the overall structure of income-earning activities in March and October, and the ways in which the average small-landowning and landless household allocated its time among them. Probing beneath these averages, I shall show how, despite major differences in the overall pattern of income-earning activities in the two periods, the allocative strategies of particular types of households exhibit important similarities.

The Wet Season Slack Period

Among the markets for male labor in March, fishpond work was by far the most attractive. Not only were the wages about 30 percent higher than those outside the village, but the duration of even relatively short-term contracts was at least as long as those offered in sugarcane and rice outside the village, and frequently longer. There are also important qualitative differences in the nature of labor relations. As mentioned in chapter 5, relationships between fishpond laborers and their employers tend toward personalized and diffuse patronage ties that provide the worker with a relatively high degree of security. For instance, fishpond workers were paid weekly and frequently obtained an advance on their wages. Labor relations in markets for sugarcane and *tebasan* rice labor were far more commercialized and generally considered demeaning; workers were closely supervised by the *penebas* (rice harvest labor contractor) or *mandur* (an official employed by the government-operated sugar industry), whereas fishpond laborers were subject to relatively little supervision.[3] Fishpond labor in March was also preferable to full-time fishing. Although average returns to fishing were relatively high, they were also highly variable; if discounted by uncertainty, they are probably at most equal to those in fishpond labor.

Seasonal patterns of participation in the fishpond labor market reflect clear class differences. Among Class III households, a group of eight to ten men, with minor variations, participated all year round in fishpond labor. In peak periods of rice production, their wages were somewhat lower than the prevailing rice labor wage, although in slack periods it was 25 to 30 percent higher than the alternatives. Although the number of Class III participants did not vary seasonally, the pattern for

3. This observation refers to those who work during the day clearing sediment from the ponds. At night, however, when fish and shrimp are being caught, the owner is often present. Day work is a far larger proportion of fishpond labor than night work.

Class II men was entirely different. In peak rice periods, there were two (or at most three) small-landowning men who worked as fishpond laborers. In slack periods, however, the number of Class II participants in fishpond labor increased sharply; in February and March, for instance, thirteen of the nineteen Class II men participating in wage labor worked as fishpond laborers. The reasons why Class II men gained preferential access to short-term fishpond labor and why wage rates did not decline despite the landless men's willingness to accept lower wages outside the village are explored in chapter 7. The more immediate question is how, given the smaller range of wage labor opportunities available to them, other men allocated their time between wage labor and fishing in March.

Part of the answer to this question lies in the internal household structure and the activity patterns of women and children. One of the most striking differences between Class II and Class III households shown in table 25 is the average proportion of wage labor undertaken by women in March. Rates of participation in wage labor by Class II adult women fell from 75 percent in December-January to 17 percent in March. Some small-landowning women switched to trading, and a large proportion gathered food and fuel for home consumption. By and large, however, Class II women did not engage in income-generating activities in March. Among Class III women, there was also a decline in labor force participation, but by far less—from 90 percent in December–January to 70 percent in March. Ten of the eleven Class III women who did not participate in wage labor in March share an interesting set of characteristics. First, nine of the ten were mothers of infants or small children; the average dependency ratio in these eleven households is 53 percent compared with the average of 30 percent for all landless households. Although the presence of small children in the household may reduce the probability of a woman's participating in wage labor outside the village, it is not a necessary condition for nonparticipation; several other landless households contained young children whose mothers maintained or increased their labor market activity in March.

The other key defining characteristic of women who did not participate in wage labor in March is that they belonged to

TABLE 25. Composition of Off-Farm Income-Earning Activities in Sukodono, March (Wet season—slack)

	Class II		Class III		Average hourly returns (Rp)	
	HOUSE-HOLD	(% FEMALE)[a]	HOUSE-HOLD	(% FEMALE)[a]	FEMALE	MALE
Wage labor inside village						
Rice	3.8	(9.7)	2.3	(71.0)	12[d]	28[d]
Fishpond	19.5	(0.0)	14.8	(0.0)	—	33
Other[b]	2.6	(0.0)	4.1	(31.8)	—	37[d]
Wage labor outside village						
Rice	8.7	(18.3)	11.2	(68.8)	24[c]	24[e]
Sugarcane	10.2	(80.0)	23.2	(90.5)	12–15[f]	26
Total wage labor	44.8	(22.6)	55.6	(56.9)		
Fishing	26.0	(0.0)	29.3	(0.0)	—	38[d]
Gathering	11.5	(45.9)	12.3	(74.2)	11	25[d]
Trading	17.7	(91.7)	2.8	(100.0)	48[d]	—
TOTAL	100.0	(31.6)	100.0	(43.2)		
Average hrs./ household	281		351			
Average hrs./ worker[c]	73		104			

[a]Refers to the proportion of household time in that activity performed by women and girls.
[b]Primarily (although not exclusively) more skilled jobs, such as house construction and repair, generally only available on a sporadic basis.
[c]Per person aged 10 and over.
[d]Indicates high variability.
[e]Separating returns to male and female workers is not meaningful because they often worked in groups; see text.
[f]The lower wage is that paid to children.

households that were economically stronger than the average for Class III. Ten of the eleven households in which adult women did not work as wage laborers in March either controlled some land, contained more than one male over the age of 14, and/or had an adult male who worked as a full-time fishpond laborer. The only one who does not conform to this general pattern is an elderly woman who was ill in March.

Women who remained in the wage labor force in March actually increased their average work duration relative to the peak season months. Much of this work was in sugarcane production, which also makes heavy use of child labor at lower wages. Despite wage rates of less than 3 cents an hour, Class III households generally responded positively to this opportunity for their children to earn income: eight of the twelve Class III girls in the 10 to 15 year age group participated in sugarcane labor, and their average work duration is almost identical to that of adult women participants.[4] A closer inspection of the internal structures of the households to which these girls belong suggests that their role in the domestic economy varied according to household size and composition. Four were the daughters of women with no husbands, and their participation in wage labor was probably compensating for the absence of an adult male. The others, however, were members of larger households, and the income that they and their mothers earned was an important factor enabling their fathers to specialize in high-risk fishing.

In most Class II and III households, men and boys did some fishing in March. In the case of men, this often involved either going fishing in the evenings after returning from wage labor or fishing full-time for a day or more between wage labor contracts. Six men in Class II and eleven in Class III spent the majority of their time fishing. The Class III men fall into two clearly defined categories; with one exception, they either have access to land or belong to large households with a high proportion of older children and a low dependency ratio. Among

4. Of the four Class III girls not participating in wage labor, three were barely 10 years old at the time of the survey and the fourth is the daughter of a fishpond laborer. Only one girl belonging to a Class II household participated in wage labor.

the landholding households, there does not seem to be any systematic relationship between men's fishing and either household structure or the activities of other household members. In the completely landless households, however, men's specializing in fishing was accompanied in each case by extensive participation of women and children in income-earning activities; work duration in these households averaged 640 hours, almost twice that of the sample as a whole. There were several other completely landless households of similar size and composition that opted for a different configuration of activities and lower average work duration, suggesting that a relatively large number of working-age members was a necessary, but not a sufficient, condition for men to specialize in fishing.

In general, these findings suggest that only households in a relatively strong economic position can engage in more lucrative activities with highly variable returns, and that the internal structure of the household can to some extent compensate for lack of physical resources in enabling certain members to engage in such activities. This type of diversification is, however, contingent on other household members—in this instance, and probably in general, women and girls—deploying considerable amounts of labor to activities that insure a constant flow of income into the household, but that typically yield extremely low returns to labor.

The relatively advantageous position of bigger Class III households with low dependency ratios is underlined if one contrasts their position with the most destitute group in the sample—the fourteen landless households comprising five in the early stages of the developmental cycle, two elderly couples with no children, and seven female-headed households. Although landless households with a large number of working-age members had to deploy part of their labor to low returns activities in order to undertake more lucrative ones, households with less favorable internal structures were completely dependent on the least remunerative opportunities. For instance, a large proportion of the time spent by Class III males in sugarcane and rice labor outside the village was undertaken by this group.

The Dry Season: Intermediate Period

An analogous pattern emerges in October in the context of a totally different set of opportunities. The overall structure of off-farm income-earning activities in October (table 26) differs from that in March in several major respects. First, wage labor opportunities increased sharply relative to fishing, which in October was almost exclusively for home consumption. Second, the composition of wage labor activities inside and outside the village underwent major changes. The level of demand for rice labor within the village was far higher than that in March, but was considerably lower than during the earlier peaks (December-January and May-June). Rice labor inside and outside the village differed not only in terms of wage rates, but also in the nature of labor arrangements. Although labor relations in rice and tobacco production within the village were generally less diffuse than the patronage ties between fishpond owners and laborers, they were considerably more personalized than those in *tebasan* rice harvesting, which comprised most of the rice labor outside the village.

How did different groups respond to this structure of opportunities? In the average Class II household, the total amount of time spent in off-farm income-earning activities was 7 percent lower than in March, compared with a 33 percent average increase in Class III. However, the wage labor involvement of both men and women in Class II increased relative to other activities and also in absolute terms; the increased supply of wage labor by small landowners also occurred concurrently with a 60 percent rise in the time that they devoted to own-production activities. The proportion of Class II women participating in wage labor rose from 17 percent in March to over 60 percent in October, and that of men from 65 percent to 75 percent.

The most significant feature of labor force participation patterns by Class II households is that 80 percent of the time that they spent in wage labor was within the village at uniformly high wage rates. In contrast, 60 percent of the wage labor undertaken by the average Class III household was in far less remunerative jobs outside the village. If one looks more closely

TABLE 26. Composition of Off-Farm Income-Earning Activities in Sukodono, October (Dry season—harvest)

	Class II		Class III		Average hourly returns (Rp)	
	HOUSE-HOLD	(% FEMALE)[a]	HOUSE-HOLD	(% FEMALE)[a]	FEMALE	MALE
Wage labor inside village						
Rice	37.3	(44.6)	19.9	(58.9)	24	39
Fishpond	13.1	(0.0)	11.3	(0.0)	—	33
Tobacco	6.6	(0.0)	3.2	(0.0)	—	39
Other	6.5	(0.0)	2.6	(0.0)	—	55[d]
Wage labor outside village						
Rice	12.1	(65.7)	38.7	(65.2)	21[c]	23[c]
Fishpond	—		2.6	(0.0)	—	30
Sugarcane	4.5	(100.0)	0.5	(50.7)	14	27
Total wage labor	80.1	(32.8)	87.0	(49.4)		
Fishing	7.4	(0.0)	1.6	(0.0)	—	21[d]
Gathering	8	(25.0)	5.1	(23.1)	11	16
Trading	10.7	(81.5)	6.1	(56.5)	40[d]	40[d]
TOTAL	100.0	(34.7)	100.0	(46.5)		
Average hrs./ household	262		466			
Average hrs./ worker[b]	68		137			

[a]Refers to the proportion of household time in that activity performed by women and girls.
[b]Per person aged 10 and over.
[c]Separating returns to male and female workers is not meaningful, because they often worked in groups; see text.
[d]Indicates high variability.

at the characteristics of Class III people who managed to gain access to jobs inside the village in October, another highly significant pattern emerges: those Class III households with access to land, together with the permanent fishpond laborers and their wives, account for 70 percent of the time that Class III households spent in jobs inside the village. The system of job rationing revealed by these figures is similar to the situation in February and March when a select group of men gained access to fishpond labor, and fishpond wage rates did not decline despite the willingness of other men to accept far lower wage rates in other wage labor activities.

The strategies adopted by those Class III household members who had to rely on jobs outside the village are also analogous to the situation in March. To understand why this is so, one needs to examine the organization of *tebasan* harvesting (described in chapter 5) which formed the primary source of employment for the majority of Class III households. In addition to cutting the rice with sickles, harvesting for a *penebas* involves threshing in the field, putting the threshed rice into sacks, and carrying it to the place where it is weighed. Payment is on a piece rate basis, and at the time of the survey was Rp 4 per kg. A key feature of *tebasan* harvesting in October was that household members almost always worked in groups, the sex and age composition of which is a major determinant of returns. Groups of workers that contained adult men or older teenage boys earned an average of Rp 25 per hour of work; the average hourly earnings of groups of women and girls was in the vicinity of Rp 19–21. Table 26 shows that women and girls performed 65 percent of the *tebasan* rice labor; men and boys only worked in rice labor outside the village together with female household members. The entry of Class III boys into the wage labor force in October was substantial; participation rates rose from 13 percent in March to over 60 percent in October, almost all of which was in *tebasan* rice labor. Participation rates among girls remained high, and in general they switched from sugarcane to *tebasan* rice labor.

Among the nineteen Class III households for which *tebasan* rice labor was the major source of employment, one can discern three distinct patterns of intrahousehold participation. First, seven households with relatively large numbers of older children deployed women, girls, and boys to *tebasan* rice labor, but in six of these households adult men did not participate in this labor market. Rather, they sought work in one of the alternative labor markets, often working for relatively short periods in a variety of different jobs. These tended to be more sporadic and required a lengthier search process but offered somewhat higher returns than *tebasan* rice labor. As in March, when the income earned by women and girls in sugarcane labor enabled men and boys to specialize in fishing, the irregularity of male employment in October was made possible by the involvement of women and children in *tebasan* rice labor.

The way in which the size and internal structure of poor households shapes the activities of household members becomes even clearer if one contrasts this pattern of participation in *tebasan* rice labor with that in households with fewer working members. Five of the six households in which adult men did work as *tebasan* laborers were ones in which children had not reached working age, and the sixth was an elderly household with no children. In all cases husband and wife worked together, the former earning lower returns than in other nonrice activities outside the village. The rationale underlying this pattern of participation lies in the joint returns to labor of men and women. A man and woman working together each earned Rp 25 per hour; if the man had worked in one of the more lucrative nonrice activites (Rp 30–32) and the woman had been able to continue working as a rice laborer, her earnings would probably have fallen to about Rp 18 per hour.[5] The average returns to an hour of household labor yielded by this set of activities (Rp 24–25) are identical to those actually earned by both participating in rice labor outside the village. Given that the demand for labor in nonrice jobs outside the village was more limited and gaining access to them more difficult, joint participation in rice labor outside the village was clearly preferable. It should be noted, however, that, if both men and women had been able to work at wage rates prevailing in rice

5. Although I did not establish this directly, it is possible that a single woman would not have been able to gain access to *tebasan* labor; in this case her only option would have been sugarcane labor, which paid Rp 14 per hour.

labor inside the village, returns to an hour of household labor would have been 30 percent higher than it actually was.

The most disadvantaged in terms of both internal structure and access to opportunities is the group of female-headed households. A few of these women, particularly those with working-age children, worked as *tebasan* rice laborers. The others were primarily involved in sugarcane labor, the least remunerative of all the female wage labor markets (table 26); in October, female-headed households accounted for most of the time spent by women and girls in sugarcane labor. The advantage of this type of work lay in relatively long duration contracts, but only the poorest females were willing to accept sugarcane wages as low as those in March.

INTERHOUSEHOLD DIFFERENCES IN ALLOCATIVE STRATEGIES

Despite the entirely different structure of activities in March and October, two clearly consistent patterns have emerged.

First is the heavy weight that the landless seem to attach to income stability. Variations in allocative behavior among landless households indicate that those containing a large number of working-age members are in a better position to take advantage of activities that offer relatively high but variable returns than those with less favorable internal structures. In spite of these differences, the organizational strategies adopted by most landless households exhibit important similarities. Although men belonging to bigger households with low dependency ratios were able to engage in comparatively risky activities, this was contingent on women and children undertaking the same type of work as those in households with a weaker internal structure.

In general, the majority of landless households displayed a far higher degree of coordination and interdependence among the activities of men, women, and children than was the case in households with some degree of control over productive assets. Landless households appeared to decide on the activities of individual members on the basis of the opportunities available to the household as a whole, and tend to opt for an integrated set of activities that, despite relatively low returns to certain members, ensure a stable flow of income into the household.

The other consistent finding is that small-landowning households systematically gained preferential access to higher-wage jobs within the village; with the notable exception of permanent fishpond workers, the majority of landless households were relegated to inferior jobs, many of which were outside the village. This differential pattern of access to wage labor was also reflected in the earnings functions.

Patterns of market dependence form an important part of the explanation for the first set of findings. In chapter 5 we saw how one of the key factors that distinguishes landless households from the majority of those with some access to land is their dependence on market-purchased foodgrains, which are subject to large and partly unpredictable price fluctuations. This would explain why, with any given set of external opportunities, a landless household would be less inclined to opt for a riskier alternative than one that could at least cover its staple food needs.[6]

The differential pattern of access to wage labor is far more difficult to explain, and it is to consideration of this question that we shall now turn.

6. According to the standard neoclassical model, the inverse relation between work duration and asset status is attributable to the landless household's preference for income over "leisure." The argument that insecurity drives the poorest households to opt for long-duration, low-wage alternatives in preference to those that offer higher but riskier returns produces the same set of inferences, and it is not possible to differentiate between the two explanations.

Part III
LABOR PROCESSES, AGRARIAN CLASS FORMATION, AND THE STATE

It is always the relationship of the owners of the conditions of production to the direct producers ... which reveals the innermost secret, the hidden basis of the entire social structure, and with it the political form of the relation of sovereignty and dependence, in short, the corresponding specific form of the state.

Marx, *Capital*

7

WAGE LABOR ARRANGEMENTS: MODES OF LABOR CONTROL

On the surface, the way in which Sukodono employers recruited and remunerated labor appears idiosyncratic, if not irrational. Why, in off-peak periods of labor demand, did they exhibit a systematic preference for small landowners over landless workers? Moreover, why did the willingness of landless laborers to accept less remunerative jobs outside the village not exert a downward pressure on wages within the village?

Similar questions underlie the debate over the national data on changing employment patterns during the first part of the 1970s. Earlier I noted how those who maintain that the rural Javanese were being induced rather than pushed out of agriculture assume that rural labor markets approximate the competitive norm fairly closely. Conversely, support for the "push" hypothesis is presumed to rest on the labor market "imperfections" responsible for wage differentials.

The issue is not simply one of wage disparities and labor market imperfections: differential wages and access to employment reflect completely different modes of recruiting, organizing, and disciplining labor. Accordingly, I shall examine the internal logic of these arrangements and establish how they are connected and coexist with one another. By shedding light on the diverse sets of relations between different workers and employers, this analysis helps identify the mechanisms of labor control embodied in different arrangements and the processes through which they change.

The central argument of this chapter is that the institutional arrangements governing the recruitment and management of labor are shaped not only by aggregate labor availability, but also by social and political forces. This analysis diverges from labor market theories that have been devised to explain similar phenomena.

DIFFERENTIAL WAGES AND ACCESS
TO EMPLOYMENT

Two competing sets of theories seek to explain why, despite some sensitivity to demand conditions, rural wages fail to adjust downward in the face of considerable involuntary unemployment. Both of these theories generate inferences about wage differentials between landowning and landless workers.

The first stems from the classical view that wages are determined by a worker's minimum subsistence requirements. In its updated version, the "efficiency wage" hypothesis posits a technically determined relationship between a worker's nutritional level and his or her work effort (Leibenstein 1957; Mazumdar 1959; Rodgers 1975; Stiglitz 1976). Given this relationship, there is a unique "efficiency wage" that minimizes the cost per unit of labor effort and determines the profit-maximizing level of employment. An unemployment equilibrium is therefore possible, because it will not pay employers to lower the wage even though laborers are willing to work for less.

The theory predicts that a monopsonist will pay landowning workers less than the landless by an amount just enough to equalize the consumption levels of all workers. Although landowners are discriminated against in terms of wages, they are employed in preference to the landless. Under competitive conditions, the cost to the employer of an "efficiency hour" will be the same for all laborers, but landowning workers will be paid higher wages because access to alternative sources of consumption renders them more productive (Bliss and Stern 1978).

On the face of it the evidence from Sukodono is consistent with the competitive version of the efficiency wage theory, but on closer inspection this explanation is highly problematic. Both the descriptive data and the earnings functions show that interclass wage differentials tend to narrow in peak periods of labor demand when conditions in the labor market are most competitive. If wages were determined by a worker's physical status, such narrowing presumably would not occur. Alternatively, one could invoke the monopsonistic version of the theory and argue that in slack periods, when large landowners and fishpond owners (who are frequently the same people) exerted a relatively high degree of control over village labor markets, they employed landed workers in preference to the landless in order to capture the productivity benefits of own consumption by small landholders. Once again, however, this type of explanation is problematic, because, if this were the case, then it should have been in the interests of employers outside the village to pay landless workers *higher* wages than small landholders receive within the village, even if the caloric expenditure required to walk to a job outside the village is excluded. When it is included, one would expect the average wage received by landless workers in jobs outside the village to be higher still.

For all the difficulties inherent in the concept, minimum subsistence requirements clearly constitute some kind of floor beneath real wages. As an explanation of wage differentials, however, the efficiency wage hypothesis is at best implausible. Although we do not have the measures of health and nutritional status needed to test the theory directly, a number of young and apparently relatively healthy landless men were among those who sought low wage work outside the village. Further, the small-landowning men who gained preferential access to jobs within the village were not notable for their youth or physique. In the case of women harvesters, the efficiency wage theory is even less credible.

The alternative explanation developed by Bardhan (1979), and aimed specifically at refuting the efficiency wage hypothesis, is couched in terms of recruitment costs. Bardhan's central thesis is that the seasonality of agricultural labor demand, particularly unpredictability of timing due to weather dependence and the high costs of delay, leads employers to place a high premium on quick and ready availability of labor: "The employer is usually keen on entering into some explicit or implicit contracts with workers about a dependable supply of labor at the right time or, at least, is aware of the significant hiring or recruitment costs to be incurred as and when such recruitment needs arise" (ibid.: 488). He proposes that employers frequently wield monopsonistic power in rural labor markets, but not enough to eliminate the recruitment cost problem. In a situation of marked seasonality, the need to apply labor on their own farms is likely to render landed workers reluctant to make a major labor force commitment at the seasonal peak; they will present the employer with higher recruitment costs and will experience lower wage rates and higher levels of unemployment than landless workers who can offer a regular and assured supply of labor.

In Sukodono I observed the opposite of Bardhan's predictions. However, his ideas about the importance of recruitment costs can be adapted to devise a story that is more consistent with the evidence. First, in some circumstances, the landless are more difficult to recruit for sporadic slack season jobs because they prefer relatively long duration contracts for which they are willing to accept lower wages. According to this explanation, small landowners are *easier* to recruit partly because of minute average farm size; though small landowners apply labor intensively on a per hectare basis, the absolute amount of time they spend working on their own farms is quite small. At the same time, access to income from own production means that they are not compelled to accept less remunerative but more stable, long-term jobs as are the landless.

Although there may be certain elements of truth in this explanation, it is at best partial. First, many of the slack season jobs to which small-landholding men had access were not only of relatively long duration but did not entail lower wages. In confirmation, the male earnings function estimates in chapter 6 show that the coefficient for the "hours worked" variable (α) is not significantly less than 1. Second, if the purpose of providing small landholders with preferential access to slack season employment were primarily to ensure their labor supply in concentrated periods of demand, then one would expect wage differentials to start narrowing by September–October when employers would have become aware that the aggregate labor demand profile was tending to flatten out; according to the recruitment cost theory, there is no apparent reason why at that point they should prefer to hire small landholders rather than the landless. Small landholders' preferential access to comparatively high wage opportunities in the village was, however, even *more* pronounced in October than it had been in March (the slack period of the wet season) when employers anticipated an extremely tight labor market situation in May–June.

MODES OF LABOR RECRUITMENT AND CONTROL

The explanation of differential wages and employment lies not simply in recruitment costs, but also in employers' needs to manage and discipline labor on a day-to-day basis. What on the surface appears to be a failure of market clearance is attributable to the coexistence of different modes of labor management, which in certain ways reinforce one another. Evidence from other village studies also shows how, despite differences in their specific forms, labor arrangements in different parts of Java share some important similarities with those observed in Sukodono.

Sukodono

As discussed in chapter 5, there are important differences in labor recruitment practices between labor markets within the village and those outside it. In intravillage rice and fishpond labor markets, workers do not openly request employment; rather they must be "invited." Particularly among large employers of rice labor, methods of recruitment varied somewhat according to the time constraint of the operation and the state of the aggregate labor market. At the peak of transplanting in the wet season when large amounts of female labor were demanded in a short period of time, most labor recruitment was contracted out to a small group of women who acted as brokers. A somewhat similar situation obtained in the case of male tasks that fell in periods of heavy labor demand; at these times, the large landowners tended to delegate recruitment and some supervision to *buruh dekat* (literally "close laborers"). In the case of activities that extended into relatively slack periods of labor demand, employers were far more selective in issuing "invitations" to work. The system of access to harvesting opportunities and the share that the harvester received were more analogous to slack period activities in that they were also contingent on invitation. In the dry season (May to October), as the spread of shorter duration rice varieties and staggered planting generated a more even profile of aggregate labor demand, the more selective system of recruitment tended to prevail. The principle of selective recruitment was even more marked in the case of fishpond laborers.

In general, worker-employer relations in sugarcane labor and *tebasan* rice harvesting outside the village tended to be far more impersonal and commercialized than in fishpond labor or rice work within the village and, in contrast to the latter, were regarded as demeaning. A central feature of sugarcane and *tebasan* labor is that prospective workers were not invited but had actively to seek jobs; particularly in periods when work opportunities were scarce, those who already had a relationship (*hubungan*) with a sugarcane supervisor (*mandur*) or harvesting broker (*penebas*) were more likely to obtain work, but such relationships did not provide anything like the security of employment available to fishpond workers or rice laborers with close connections to the village elite.

To explain these different patterns, I shall consider, first, the specific organizational and technological factors that influence strategies of labor recruitment and management. In the case of sugarcane, the *mandurs* (supervisors) are employees of the government-operated sugar mills. Because the total labor costs of cultivating a particular area of cane are prespecified, the *mandur* in effect has a free hand in recruitment and wage determination; thus, he stands to profit substantially from minimizing wages. Furthermore, the *mandurs* have a strong incentive to exercise constant and close monitoring, because retaining their own jobs is contingent on delivering a satisfactory yield. The distinguishing characteristic of *tebasan* harvesting labor is that output is easily monitored and piece rate payments can thus be used to ensure effort.

In contrast, the major village employers were in a position where exercising direct supervision was both costly and impractical. The fishponds are a substantial distance from the village, and the daytime task of shovelling silt is continuous. As far as rice is concerned, modern rice technology enhances the importance of such activities as water control, fertilizer and pesticide application, and weeding, which are far less easily observable than standard tasks such as land preparation, transplanting, and harvesting.

Probably the more important component in the higher cost of direct supervision faced by the large village employers was their opportunity cost, defined by the wide range of lucrative alternatives available to them. The extremely time-consuming political activities in which the elite are involved form an essential precondition for maintaining positions of power within the village and for gaining access to the resources of the state. Similarly, the growing involvement of wealthier groups in trading and brokerage activities—many of them outside the village—creates incentives for indirect methods of labor management.

Those who gained preferential access to jobs within the village are distinguished not only (or even exclusively) by landownership, but also by other forms of relations with their employers. There are two distinct groups. The first consists of fishpond laborers—both permanent landless workers and a group of small landholders employed in off-peak periods of rice production—who received interest-free credit in the form of wage advances. In the second group are borrowers who repay their loans by sharecropping on their own land. At yields and prices prevailing at the time of the survey, returns to the lender were in the vicinity of 100 to 150 percent per cropping season. Although these forms of indebtedness were highly extractive, there were other dimensions to the relationship between borrower and lender. In several instances, debtor-sharecroppers were employed as wage laborers by their creditors on somewhat better terms than were available outside the village.

The rationale underlying labor arrangements within the village starts to emerge more clearly when one examines the characteristics of workers involved in these arrangements. A closer look reveals that the two sets of households constitute distinctively different social groups. An important indication of these differences lies in residential patterns. The residential area of the village is divided into four contiguous "blocks," with the two northerly sections (blocks 3 and 4) comprising the "upper class"

area of the village. These divisions are reflected in landownership patterns: the proportion of large-landholding, small-
landholding, and landless households in blocks 3 and 4 is 70
percent, 55 percent, and 35 percent, respectively, with all but
one of the wealthiest households (those with more than one
hectare) living in block 4. This pattern in turn reflects the history of village settlement. Those living in blocks 3 and 4 are by
and large descendants of the original settlers; relative newcom-
ers—many of them landless—tended to settle in the southerly
area. The significance of this is that both small-landowning and
landless households in blocks 3 and 4 are far more likely to
have long-standing social ties with the village elite, which in
some cases probably extend to kinship relations. A particularly
striking pattern is that all but one of the thirteen small-
landholding men who gained access to fishpond work were
residents of blocks 3 and 4; furthermore, *all* of the full-time
landless fishpond laborers lived in this part of the village. In
contrast, about 85 percent of the households involved in land-
credit arrangements were in blocks 1 and 2, and they comprised over 70 percent of the small-landholding households in
this area.

   In seeking to explain why fishpond owners gave preferential
treatment to workers with whom they had long-standing social
ties, a point that suggests itself is that it is not just the duration
or personal nature of employers' relations with their workers
that enhances labor discipline, but also the implicit sanctions
that employers can bring to bear. On the one hand, the pater-
nalistic and comparatively generous terms of fishpond contracts rendered the worker highly dependent on the employer;
on the other, these relations of dependency were more effective
when applied to workers who had more to lose. One aspect of
this dependence is that the prospect of being thrown into the
"open" segment of the labor market is likely to be far more
threatening to a higher-status worker than it would be to one
who has already had to cope with it. Further, it is not only the
identity of the employer and worker vis-à-vis one another that
matters; one of the key differences between workers living in
blocks 3 and 4 and those from the lower-class area of the village

is that some sort of blacklisting could far more easily be applied to the former. Precisely because of their somewhat higher status, the fishpond workers were more vulnerable to sanctions and therefore more amenable to indirect methods of labor management.

Those tied into land-debt arrangements are a completely separate group whose relations with their employers are quite different from those of the fishpond workers. In assessing why it could be in the interests of the creditor-landlord to provide the indebted household with preferential access to employment, the key point is that the primary determinant of returns to the lender is yields. In principle, therefore, these arrangements are highly risky. The lender's risk lies in the possibility that the owner-borrower-sharecropper will undersupply labor (as well as other inputs) and thereby produce lower than optimum yields. This provides an important clue as to why it could be in the interests of the lender to provide preferential access to employment. In having to hand over two-thirds of its output, the indebted household becomes heavily dependent on outside sources of income and will tend to seek out a stable source of employment. The possibility of this being successful poses a substantial danger to the lender. However, the lender's ability to offer employment opportunities and to regulate the timing of such work provides a powerful means of ensuring that the undersupplying of labor, which is likely to accompany the sharecropper-debtor's finding outside employment, does not occur; by holding out the prospect of more favorable employment opportunities than the sharecropping household is likely to find elsewhere, the lender is better able to control the deployment of labor by the household and thereby ensure returns to capital.

From the viewpoint of the debtor-sharecropper, the security that these arrangements provide is likely to be of central importance. This consideration assumes added significance when one recalls that the vast majority of small-landowning households involved in land-credit arrangements are from the "lower-class" section of the village, and therefore lack the close social ties that provide the fishpond workers with preferential access to work. When viewed from this perspective, the land-credit arrangements—most of which had been contracted since the early 1970s—appear as a comparatively harsh form of patronage, which nevertheless provide a modicum of security.

A defining characteristic of these arrangements is, of course, that landless workers were automatically excluded. The availability of sugarcane labor meant that the poorest groups did not, by and large, have to resort to scavenging on the scale that was observed in other Javanese villages during the 1970s (White 1979). Nonetheless, the low-wage and generally demeaning character of jobs outside the village, together with the large number of landless men, women, and children willing to accept them, formed an essential precondition for the hiring strategies of the major employers in Sukodono; in particular, it allowed them to use the provision of job security as an indirect means of organizing and disciplining labor. The chief consequence of Sukodono employers' taking advantage of the inferior options and weak bargaining power of labor was a growing division within the work force. Underlying the wage differentials described in chapter 6 is a process of structural differentiation between those incorporated into more complex arrangements and those relegated to the "open" segment of the wage labor market and less remunerative types of nonagricultural self-employment.

One of the most obvious reasons why these arrangements had emerged in Sukodono was that the village had been closed off to the purchase of land by outsiders (chapter 4). The village elite thereby gained monopolistic control over the land market through the medium of indebtedness and were able to extend their access to land, while simultaneously strengthening their control over labor. In turn, probably the main reason why the headman had managed to seal off the village was its reputation of being politically "safe"; villages in which the Indonesian Communist party was active in the early 1960s are far more susceptible to outside intervention. Although the institutional arrangements in Sukodono were shaped by a historically specific set of local circumstances, they are similar in several important ways to the arrangements that were emerging in another village.

Gondosari

Gondosari, a village studied by Husken (1979), is also located on the northern coastal plain of central Java. Land concentration is, however, far more pronounced than in Sukodono. Only a third of the village households own land, more than half of which is controlled by a small group of large landowners who comprise about 4 percent of the total village households. Among the large number of landless Gondosari households, Husken identifies two groups of roughly equal size: those who are involved in sharecropping and related contracts known elsewhere in Java as *kedokan* or *ceblokan;* and those who sell labor rather indifferently to a number of employers on a short-term basis and supplement their agricultural wage earnings with various nonagricultural self-employment activities—mat weaving, broom making, gathering firewood, selling food, and other forms of petty trade—that yield extremely low returns. Sharecroppers and *kedokan* workers are, according to Husken, in a far better position than those who must piece together a livelihood from a variety of sources.

The dominant sharecropping arrangement in the village requires the tenant to cultivate modern rice varieties and apply appropriate levels of fertilizer and pesticides; nonlabor-input costs are shared on the basis of two-thirds to the landlord and one-third to the tenant (*morotelu*). The labor arrangement that seems to be expanding most rapidly is one in which the worker performs all tasks except plowing and harrowing and receives one-ninth to one-twelfth of the yield, while the owner covers all input costs. According to Husken, this form is "operated above all by the most 'entrepreneurial' farmers" who tend also to be those who gain access to inputs on the most favorable terms.

This contract is a particular instance of a general category of arrangement known as *kedokan* that has been spreading rapidly in different parts of Java. The institution is, however, an old one:[1]

The word "*kedok*" actually means a dyked-off section of a sawah (wet rice field), one of the squares in the great chess-board effect

---

1. In the area studied by van der Kolff, *kedokan* was said to have first been practiced in the late nineteenth century.

presented by an extensive irrigated rice field. The system of that name is one whereby an agreement is entered into between the owner of the ground and some second party amounting to this, that in one or more sections or *kedoks* the latter agrees to attend to certain definite jobs against payment in the form of a fraction of the product that is grown on the land he works. This system is differentiated from that of share tenancy . . . in that in the latter case *all* the work done on the particular piece of ground must be done by the tenant. (Van der Kolff 1936: 17)

Although the tasks specified in a *kedokan* contract vary, the general pattern seems to be that the owner takes responsibility for land preparation activities that require draft animals.

As far as the worker is concerned, at any given level of pay a *kedokan* contract has several clear disadvantages relative to wage labor. First, the worker has to bear part of the risk of harvest failure. This is obviously advantageous to the employer, in that labor costs are scaled proportionately according to output. The second drawback of *kedokan* from the viewpoint of the worker is that it entails a highly uneven flow of income. Accordingly, in order to enter into a *kedokan* contract, a worker must have access to other sources of income in the period preceding the harvest; this could require borrowing, which may or may not form part of a *kedokan* contract. In the event that it does, the worker's income would obviously be reduced by the amount of the interest payments. Counterposed against these drawbacks, the primary nonwage benefit that a *kedokan* contract conveys on a worker is job security. There are two interrelated parts to this. First, within a given cropping cycle the worker has assured access to work, even though the exact amount of labor income is uncertain. Second is the possibility that the contract will be renewed over successive cropping seasons.[2]

In a tight labor market situation, *kedokan* contracts are likely to be comparatively expensive to employers. Workers will attach relatively little value to job security per se, and employers will have to compensate them for the more negative features of *kedokan*. At the same time, as their opportunity costs rise, workers are likely to expend less effort on any given *kedok*. In con-

2. Soentoro et al. report that *kedokan* contracts are generally renewed with the same tenant (1981).

trast, limited outside employment opportunities together with large supplies of labor operate so as to enhance the attractiveness of *kedokan* contracts, both to workers and employers. In such conditions, workers will attach substantially greater value to job security. To the extent that this outweighs the nonwage disadvantages, *kedokan* contracts will tend to become cheaper than short-term wage labor arrangements that offer no job security. By the same token, the more highly workers value job security, the greater the effort they are likely to expend on a particular *kedok* in order to ensure renewal of the contract. In order for the labor management mechanism to operate to greatest effect, available work opportunities must be concentrated within a particular group of workers rather than being spread evenly among all those available.[3] By placing *kedokan* workers in a comparatively privileged position relative to a pool of underemployed workers, such a division enhances the value of job security and thereby facilitates labor management.

A second important characteristic of *kedokan* is that, by adding extra tasks to the contract with no corresponding increase in the harvest share, employers can readily lower wages.[4] Moreover, in the process of requiring additional tasks the employer is likely to gain access to the labor of additional household members. A "minimal" *kedokan* contract in which access to the harvest is confined to those who have transplanted without pay is almost always an exclusively female arrangement. If, however, land preparation tasks are added, then the contract comes to encompass the entire household. Van der Kolff describes how this process led to a shift in the balance of power within the household:

> With the inclusion of digging in the work to be done there came an alteration in the way in which the contract was made. Since the work had to begin with male labor, it was no longer the woman but

3. This point is developed in more general analytical terms by Stoft (1982).

4. Van der Kolff reports that in areas where *kedokan* took hold, the tendency was for additional tasks to be added to the contract. He describes one of the ways in which owners persuaded workers to perform extra tasks: "The solicitant was faced with the choice of applying this original system [i.e., transplanting and weeding in addition to harvesting] on a small patch in which he could plant out no more than ten bunches from the nursery beds, or of doing far more work on a more extensive area" (1936: 24).

the man who came to negotiate with the *sawah* owner. The results of the discussions were then passed on to the wives of both parties so that they could keep them in mind when arranging their program of work (1936: 24).

Although adding extra tasks amounts to lowering wages, it also signifies enhanced employment security for those households that participate in *kedokan*. At the same time, by concentrating work opportunities, it exacerbates the insecurity of those that are excluded.

Precisely such a process of work concentration was taking place in Gondosari. Although the terms of sharecropping and *kedokan* contracts were tending to move against workers, they were superior to the alternatives of sporadic wage labor and nonagricultural self-employment: "Aware that numerous other landless are ready to step into his [*sic*] place, the sharecropper [*kedokan* worker] has no choice but to conform to the new demands upon him" (Husken 1979: 148). By the same token, these arrangements enable the landlord/employer "to devote his time to other things (trade, village politics, leisure), because he can confine himself to a few instructions and an occasional visit to the *sawahs* (wet rice fields) to inspect the crops" (ibid.: 149).

Herein lies the essential similarity between *kedokan* and the institutional forms observed in Sukodono. Although the latter operated primarily via land-credit arrangements and the *kedokan* contracts described by Husken are a more direct means of reducing labor costs, the underlying principles of labor management that they embody are fundamentally similar. The key characteristic shared by both sets of arrangements is that, by providing the worker with job security, the employer is better able to exercise control. The effectiveness of these measures is, however, crucially contingent on the existence of a pool of underemployed workers, while in turn contributing to it. Husken observes that, in Gondosari:

> The agricultural labourers have seen only the negative effects of this transition to rural capitalism, namely a drastic decrease in employment as the rationalization of rice and peanut production on the lands of large landowners where they used to work has grad-

ually resulted in the expulsion of their "superfluous" labor. In the absence of any other employment prospects they are increasingly driven into the marginal sectors of the village economy such as petty trade, various forms of handicrafts and cottage-industry and the illegal felling and selling of teak wood from the government forest. Such forms of activity generally provide much lower returns to labour. (1979: 149)

This process is, of course, closely analogous to that whereby landless workers in Sukodono were being relegated to the "open" segment of the labor market and less remunerative forms of self-employment.

Another similarity between the arrangements in Sukodono and Gondosari is that both involve workers' paying what is in effect an employment fee. In the case of *kedokan*, the worker's only receiving payment at harvest time amounts to a loan to the employer equivalent to the preharvest wages bill. The worker receives interest to the extent that the share exceeds the wages bill for an equivalent amount of day labor. Any discrepancy between that interest rate and the "prevailing" one could be regarded as an employment fee. Similarly, one could argue that the extremely high interest rates being paid by those involved in the land-credit arrangements in Sukodono were in part a fee for access to employment.

The chief difference is that the land-credit arrangements in Sukodono were creating a split along the lines of landownership and landlessness, whereas the sharecropping contracts observed in Gondosari were tending to divide the landless into two distinct groups. These differences stem partly from the extreme concentration of landownership in Gondosari, which meant that, in contrast to the situation in Sukodono, a small-landowning peasantry was largely absent. As noted earlier, an important additional reason why the land-credit arrangements had emerged in Sukodono was the ban on sales of land to outsiders, which reflected the particular political history of the village. The consequences were, however, essentially the same, namely, a division within the work force between those with preferential access to work and income and those whose position was far more tenuous.

Evidence From Other Village Studies

The key similarity shared by the institutional arrangements just discussed is that they involve providing a select group of workers with job security. Accordingly, slack labor market conditions are a necessary condition for these types of arrangements although they are far from sufficient.

The strategy of managing workers by selectively extending "privileges" is more general and can obtain in tight labor market conditions as well as in slack ones. This point is well illustrated by a study of a western Javanese village in which there had been a particularly marked tightening in the labor market as a consequence of irrigation improvements together with a decline in the number of migrants coming into the village (Kasryno et al. 1982). Between 1971 and 1981, average real agricultural wages rose by about 25 percent. Although total labor input per hectare remained virtually unchanged, labor use in land preparation fell sharply as a result of mechanization; by 1981 ten farmers owned power tillers, and virtually all the land preparation in the village was done with power tillers on a contract basis.

Among the large landowners, important changes in labor hiring had also taken place, which involved the emergence of a group of permanent agricultural laborers:

> During the wet season crop, landless laborers worked as permanent agricultural laborers with daily wage payment. The laborers in the wet season were engaged in every phase of rice production; even the wife of the laborer took part in this work especially in the transplanting, weeding and harvesting. In the dry season when yields were substantially lower the laborers became tenants through a sharecropping contract. In addition, landowners extended credit for the dry season production expenses as well as living expenses for the tenants. (Kasryno et al. 1982: 105)

The rather small group of households involved in these arrangements was substantially better off than the landless and small-landowning households that combined casual agricultural wage labor with nonagricultural self-employment. Kasryno et al. estimate that the annual per capita income of a permanent-labor household—none of which engaged in nonagricultural work—was in the vicinity of 30 percent above that of the average landless or near-landless household.

There are clear parallels among *kedokan*, the arrangements in Sukodono, and the types of arrangements observed by Kasryno et al. The key similarity is that, by selectively extending "privileges" to particular workers, employers are better able to manage them. As aggregate labor market conditions tighten, job security becomes ineffective and the "inducements" that employers use to ensure an adequate and disciplined labor force become more costly. The basic principle of labor management is, however, similar, as is the labor market segmentation to which this type of strategy gives rise.

Clearly, however, a number of important questions remain unanswered. For instance, do slack labor market conditions necessarily give rise to indirect forms of labor management based on job security, and, if not, why? What determines the form of the institutional arrangement, and who gets recruited? The answers to these and a host of other questions lie in a better understanding of employers' needs to exercise social control. By the same token, though aggregate labor market conditions shape the nature and costs of the "privileges" that employers use in order to regulate the labor process, they do not form a sufficient basis for understanding the structure of institutional arrangements.

Nevertheless, certain hypotheses can be advanced about the way in which changes in labor market conditions are likely to influence the forms of institutional arrangements. An extremely important example is the shift from staggered to synchronized planting, which gives rise to a sharper seasonal profile of labor demand. For brief, transitory periods, the bargaining power of labor is enhanced, and this tends to undermine *kedokan* arrangements. Workers are unlikely to be willing to forego preharvest wages when there is a heavy demand for harvest labor concentrated in a short period. From the employer's point of view, greater seasonality in the aggregate profile of labor demand undermines the usefulness of job security as an instrument of labor management because it raises the opportunity cost of labor at precisely the time that the employer is most concerned that the worker supply maximum effort.

Consistent with these arguments, there is also evidence of a decline in *kedokan* associated with greater synchronization of planting (White and Makali 1979: 32; Kasryno et al. 1982: 37). These patterns bear directly on the interpretation of aggregate wage data and their distributional implications.

THE TRANSFORMATION OF AGRARIAN LABOR ARRANGEMENTS

A notable feature of *kedokan* arrangements is their tendency to disappear and reappear, sometimes with astonishing speed. The classic example is provided by van der Kolff, who found that in 1922, when the Javanese economy was experiencing a major boom, "precapitalist" forms, such as *kedokan*, apparently were giving way to wage labor paid in cash (1936). When he returned to the same area in the depths of the depression in 1936, however, there had been a sharp increase in *kedokan* and "people were unanimous in sounding its praise":

> I was informed that the drawback upon which such stress was laid in early years, viz. the being late with the operations, needed not to be dreaded. They answered in opposition that after all the work of the occupier is controlled by the owner. If the man [sic] is inclined to be lazy, he incurs the displeasure of his employer and will run the risk of not being accepted as a *kedok* tenant anywhere again. (ibid.: 48)

Recently and on a fairly large scale, *kedokan* appears to have reemerged after a period of decline (White and Makali 1979: 17). In a survey of 589 villages in the Cimanuk Basin area of West Java, Wiradi (1978) found that *kedokan* was practiced in two-thirds of the villages. Between 1970 and 1975, *kedokan* expanded in some villages and declined in others; there was, nevertheless, a net expansion that was particularly marked in rice villages, where the increase was twice as rapid as the decline. A significant finding by Wiradi is that the expansion of *kedokan* seemed unrelated to the spread of modern rice varieties. A later study by Hayami and Hafid confirmed the recent spread of *kedokan* in other areas of West Java (1979). Although the incidence of *kedokan* may be highest in West Java, increases have also been reported in Central and East Java (Soentoro et al. 1981; Husken 1979; Hayami and Kikuchi 1982). The significance of expanding *kedokan* arrangements is that, by conveying exclusive harvesting rights, they generally signify a process through which the number of people who have access to both harvesting opportunities and preharvest labor is declining.

Technological and Demographic Explanations

As discussed in chapter 1, the most widely held view is that these changes reflect a disintegration of traditional poverty sharing, brought about by the Green Revolution. According to this view, technologically induced commercialization has caused large farmers to renege on their customary obligations to provide poor villagers with income opportunities. The rationale seems to be that the use of purchased inputs associated with the new technology engenders a profit-maximizing mentality on the part of employers and is accompanied by a shift from "traditional" to "commercial" determination of labor use.

The most obvious problem with this view is that there does not seem to be any consistent relationship between technological change and the expansion of institutions tending to exclude workers from agriculture. This inconsistency is apparent both from the large-scale evidence report by Wiradi (1978) and from village studies.[5] Further, there is evidence that the closing of harvests often predated the advent of modern rice technology (Hayami and Hafid 1979).

An alternative explanation is that the spread of such institutions as *kedokan* is a reflection of population growth in the face of stagnant technology. The main proponents of this view (Hayami and Kikuchi 1982) contend that these institutions enable employers to reduce wages and simultaneously uphold "traditional village norms." In support of this argument, they adduce evidence from a western Javanese village that was ecologically unsuited to modern rice technology. Rice harvesters in the village had formerly been paid a one-seventh share. The

---

5. Compare, e.g., Husken (1979) and Hayami and Kikuchi (1982).

hourly wage rate implicit in this share (Rp 84) was considerably higher than the prevailing wage rate for preharvest labor (Rp 60). According to Hayami and Kikuchi's calculations, a switch to a *kedokan* contract, which requires the worker to transplant and weed in addition to harvesting though still receiving a one-seventh share of output, reduces the implicit hourly wage for all operations to precisely Rp 60. A similar wage reduction could in principle have been accomplished either by paying lower cash wages for harvesting or by reducing harvest shares. According to the authors, the former was rejected because "the cost of resistance to change in long-established custom in the village community would have been quite large" (ibid.: 188). Similarly,

> the reduction of the share rate was not quite so consistent with basic village moral principles such as mutual help and income-sharing. In terms of patron-client relationships in a village community characterized by multi-stranded ties, it would have involved less social friction to add some additional obligations while maintaining the same share rate. (ibid.)

The argument that shifting from a relatively open harvest-share system to *kedokan* avoids social friction is questionable, however, because it involves conveying exclusive harvesting rights on *kedokan* workers and thereby circumscribing the income opportunities available to others. Boedhisantoso has observed that the exclusionary mechanism of *kedokan* arrangements can entail high social costs:

> The exclusive right to harvest is an expensive privilege, materially as well as spiritually. The holder may suffer from social isolation in his own village community by being condemned as greedy or anti-social by his fellow villagers, who are themselves fighting for their day-to-day livelihood from limited opportunities to work. Likewise although by maintaining a *ceblok* or *ngawesi* [i.e., *kedokan*] relationship a wealthy landowner may acquire greater material benefits, he is likely to lose popularity as a result. Sometimes he becomes the target (*bulan-bulanan*) of his poorer fellow-villagers, with the risk of greater loss or damage to his rice crops. (1976: 24)

Another problem with Hayami and Kikuchi's interpretation of *kedokan* is that it cannot explain the suddenness with which *kedokan* appeared; according to the authors, the incidence of *kedokan* in the hamlet that they studied jumped from 27 percent in 1964–1965 to 52 percent in 1966–1967, and had reached 96 percent by 1978 (Hayami and Kikuchi 1982: table 8-10). If, as they assert, the main reason why *kedokan* emerged as the dominant form was because it was the most morally acceptable way of reducing wage rates in response to population growth, there is no apparent reason why these reductions were executed with such rapidity.

An Alternative Explanation of Structural Change

The transformation of labor arrangements can only be understood in the context of the massive political and administrative changes that have taken place since the mid-1960s. Chapter 2 described the increasingly open antagonism between large landowners and the landless in the late Sukarno period associated with the PKI's strategy of mobilizing the poor peasantry. The landowning elite were confronted not only by threats of land appropriation and insurrection, but also by the disintegration of bureaucratic authority. At the same time, their control over rice placed them in an extremely powerful position with the mega-inflation and severe food shortages that prevailed in the first part of the 1960s. Virtually no direct evidence exists on the forms of agrarian relations during this period. There is every reason to suppose, however, that the combined effects of political mobilization, inflation, and bureaucratic disintegration must have been profound. One possible outcome is that landowners had little option other than to permit widespread access to harvesting rights. Accordingly, the comparatively high incidence of open harvests prior to 1966–1967 (Hayami and Hafid 1979; Hayami and Kikuchi 1982) may have been a reflection not so much of traditional poverty-sharing norms, but a defensive effort on the part of landowners to maintain social control over poorer groups who were both politically mobilized and in a precarious position in terms of food.

The rural upheavals of the early to mid-1960s played an important role in shaping the composition, character, and objectives of the New Order regime and the nature of its relations with the peasantry. Agrarian policy under the New Order has been marked by two clearly defined objectives: preventing the resurgence of rural unrest and expanding rice production. The major measures implemented in order to restore and maintain "law and order" in the countryside have been the vast strengthening and militarization of the bureaucracy, together with extinguishing most forms of political activity at the village level.

Even though the general pattern in the earlier stages of the New Order was one of subordination of the peasantry as a whole, the political-administrative reforms almost by definition operated so as to relieve the rural elite of the constraints to which they were subject during the late Sukarno period and simultaneously to circumscribe the bargaining power of the rural poor. When viewed in this context, the sudden expansion of such institutions as *kedokan* is clearly comprehensible. As one of Husken's respondents observed, "Previously, in the *zaman abang* (i.e., the 'red era' between 1955 and 1965 when the communist peasant union and women's movement had a big following in the village) the women received far too much. Then we couldn't do anything about it. But now everything is back to normal" (Husken 1979: 146).

Although the political-administrative changes instituted by the New Order brought about an abrupt shift in the constraints confronting different rural groups, a more gradual process of structural change was also set in motion. The chief mechanism is the way in which the the relationship of the rural elite to the state apparatus has been transformed over the course of the New Order regime. Although the state's initial efforts to force the cultivation of modern rice varieties and maintain low rice prices generated major conflicts of interest with the landed elite, substantial modifications in agrarian policy have since occurred, which in large part reflect a process through which the state has had to accommodate to the interests of the rural elite and simultaneously maintain control over them. This group remains subordinate to supravillage authorities and their ability to exert direct influence on the policy process remains heavily circumscribed, but the tendency since the early 1970s has been

toward the transformation of the rural elite into a class of favored clients of the state. Consequently, although those in positions of power at the village level have become increasingly
dependent on the state apparatus for attaining and maintaining their positions, they have also gained access to significant
opportunities for accumulation, both within and outside agriculture.

This process of incorporation of the rural elite into the
larger system forms an important part of the explanation of
changing social relations within village society. In the first place,
the strengthening of political and economic links beyond the
village has intensified the rural elite's need for a reliable and
easily managed agricultural labor force. Comparatively wealthy
and influential rural households are frequently involved in a
diverse range of nonagricultural and political activities. In the
case of Sukodono, men belonging to the upper 10 percent of
village households invariably devote large amounts of time to
maintaining and strengthening their relationships with supravillage authorities, as well as to various trading and brokerage
activities. In more "open" villages where people not formerly
involved in agriculture have acquired land, the degree of diversification among dominant groups is probably even greater. To
the extent that the major employers of agricultural labor are
being drawn into relatively lucrative nonagricultural activities
of various kinds, the costs of their direct supervision of agricultural labor are likely to be high and rising. By the same token,
accumulation within agriculture tends to depend increasingly
on cheap and effective methods of labor management. Thus,
the changing position of the rural elite in the larger system has
generated both the incentives and the resources and opportunities for redefining labor arrangements.

8

AGRARIAN CHANGE IN JAVA

What has been happening in rural Java? What are the processes that underlie these changes? What does the future hold, particularly if oil revenues stay at current levels or continue to decline?

The wider importance of the Sukodono study stems not from the direct evidence per se, but rather from the way in which the evidence sheds light on the processes at work within rural society and the relationship of these processes to the larger system. Exclusionary labor arrangements are a clear illustration of the links between macro political-economic forces and modes of labor recruitment and control at the local level. The general implication of my analysis in chapter 7 is that contractual arrangements cannot be understood purely as labor market phenomena: in order to explain variations and changes in institutional arrangements, not only the aggregate labor market, but also the social and political relations among different rural groups and the forces that shape these relations must be considered.

EXCLUSIONARY LABOR ARRANGEMENTS

The chief characteristics of the arrangements observed in Sukodono are that they are designed to keep labor cheap *and* manageable by providing job security to a select group of workers and at the same time reproducing the conditions of insecurity for others. Indeed, the effectiveness of job security as an instrument of labor discipline is crucially contingent on the existence of a pool of "underemployed" workers, while in turn contributing to it.

Institutional arrangements in Sukodono have been shaped by a specific set of local conditions, but the functions that they fulfill and their consequences are similar in several respects to the changing labor arrangements in many other parts of Java. In particular, the Sukodono arrangements are closely analogous to an attenuated form of sharecropping known as *kedokan* (or *ceblokan*), which is widely practiced in a number of areas and increased rapidly in the late 1960s. The underlying principles of labor management embodied in *kedokan* arrangements are essentially similar to those in Sukodono: by providing a select group of workers with job security and simultaneously excluding others, the employer is able to exercise indirect control over the labor process. This strategy in turn gives rise to a division between those who are involved in comparatively secure contractual arrangements and those whose position in the labor market is far more tenuous.

Slack labor market conditions are a prerequisite for exclusionary arrangements predicated on job security, but the general principle of selectively extending benefits in order to manage the labor process can obtain in tight as well as in slack labor market conditions. As aggregate labor market conditions tighten, job security per se loses its value, and employers are obliged to extend more substantive benefits (such as subsidized credit) in order to ensure both an adequate and a disciplined work force. As with job security, the more selectively these benefits are applied, the more effective they are likely to be in creating and maintaining relations of dependency and in manipulating workers' behavior. Accordingly, the state of the labor market determines the nature and costs of the "privileges" with which employers seek to exercise control over the labor process, but aggregate labor market conditions do not provide a *sufficient* basis for explaining the particular forms of institutional arrangements.

In general, the strategies that employers use to recruit, organize, and discipline labor are shaped not only by labor supply and demand, but also by power relations at the national and local level. The clearest illustration of this point is the reasons for the sudden increase in *kedokan* and other exclusionary arrangements in the late 1960s in many parts of Java. In particular, Hayami and Kikuchi's explanation (1982)—that the spread of *kedokan* is attributable to population growth in the face of stagnant technology—fails to explain the rapidity with which *kedokan* arrangements appeared (and perhaps reappeared). The more common explanation, which views technologically induced commercialization as the primary causal mechanism, is incapable of explaining the pattern of variation among villages.

An alternative hypothesis is that the sudden rise in exclusionary arrangements was intimately linked with the massive political-administrative transformation brought about by the New Order regime in the late 1960s. The rationale derives from the foregoing analysis of indirect labor management and, in particular, the exclusionary mechanisms that are essential features of *kedokan*-type arrangements. I suggest that, in the early to mid-1960s, the PKI's strategy of mobilizing the poor peasantry tended to undermine *kedokan* arrangements. In some areas, it appears that Gerwani (the women's organization of the PKI) managed to outlaw *kedokan*.[1] Even where this did not happen, the internal characteristics of *kedokan* and related arrangements are such that they are less likely to occur in conditions where political mobilization enhances the relative bargaining power of workers. When employers are subject to organized pressure from below, exclusionary strategies are simply less feasible. In these circumstances, the open harvests, which seem to have prevailed throughout the first part of the 1960s, can be seen not simply as a "traditional" poverty-sharing institution, but as a defensive effort on the part of large landowners to maintain social stability.

Viewing labor arrangements in this way offers a clear explanation of why the type of clamping down on agrarian organization that occurred in the late 1960s was accompanied by a sudden rise in *kedokan*. The militarization of the bureaucracy and the depoliticization at the village level contained any threat of organized reaction from below and thereby facilitated the

1. This point was made by Benjamin White at the Social Science Research Council conference on Everyday Forms of Peasant Resistance, The Hague, December 1982.

emergence of arrangements that enhanced labor discipline by extending preferential terms to some workers and deliberately excluding others. The subsequent shifts in the position of dominant rural groups have operated in many instances to perpetuate these types of arrangements.

This approach illustrates the importance of viewing labor arrangements in terms not only of labor management, but also social control. This perspective in turn contributes to the analysis of institutional change. In the first place, it underlines the need for examining how both macroeconomic and political forces influence the interaction between labor management and social control. Second, viewing labor arrangements in this way allows us to see institutional change as a response to changing external conditions, and also as a process through which particular institutions give rise to opposing tensions and contradictions. For example, an institution like *kedokan* appears in the first instance to be self-reinforcing, because it operates to sustain the reserve labor pool on which it rests. Its very success can, however, generate and intensify social tensions, which tend to undermine it.

Precisely such an occurrence is reported by Boedhisantoso in the northern Krawang area of West Java, who writes that *kedokan* was officially prohibited in this area in 1969 "to prevent the social tensions which might arise out of such monopolistic privileges" (1976: 24). This area is one of the most fertile and productive in Java, but it is surrounded to the south and east by regions of much lower agricultural potential. Particularly during planting and harvesting periods, huge numbers of itinerant workers swarm into northern Krawang. The banning of *kedokan* was clearly a response to the security threat posed by denying work to the unusually large volume of migrant labor surging into the area. By banning *kedokan*, the state was acting in the long-run interests of the rural elite, although in the short run the ban was clearly to their disadvantage. What this example illustrates is that, though exclusionary labor arrangements are contingent on the state's exercising social control, the spread of these arrangements can generate tensions, which in turn give rise to further change.

TRENDS IN EMPLOYMENT AND INCOME
DISTRIBUTION

The questions posed by the macro data on employment and
income distribution extend beyond the debate over whether labor was being pushed or pulled out of agriculture during the
first part of the 1970s. The pattern of employment growth appears to have been reversed in the late 1970s and early 1980s.
During this period, which coincided with large increases in oil
revenues, more decentralized government spending, and several years of bumper rice crops, the growth of agricultural employment (especially for women) increased rapidly, while nonagricultural employment for both men and women seems to
have declined sharply.

More recent data go part of the way toward resolving what
was happening over the first part of the 1970s, but they also
call attention to some important questions about the underlying mechanisms of these changes. The decline in nonagricultural employment in the boom period of the late 1970s and
early 1980s is inconsistent with the argument that the expansion of nonagricultural activities over the first part of the 1970s
was primarily a reflection of labor's being drawn into activities
stimulated by rapid economic growth. This inconsistency reflects the inadequacy of the neoclassical framework to deal with
dynamic processes. The source of the inconsistency is the pre-
sumption that returns to labor in nonagricultural activities approximate "the" agricultural wage, which in turn derives from
the assumption of perfectly competitive labor markets.

An alternative interpretation, which is not only internally
consistent but which is also supported by a good deal of micro
data, is that important shifts in the composition of nonagricultural activities took place in the late 1970s. According to this
interpretation, a sizable proportion of the expansion in nonagricultural activities over the first part of the 1970s was in marginal nonagricultural rural activities, many of which yielded
lower returns to labor than those in agriculture.[2] The apparent

2. Summarizing the evidence from village studies conducted over the first part of
the 1970s, White observes that

Landless, near-landless, and small-farm and large-farm households obtain significant proportions of their income from non-agricultural activities, but it must be

decline in the growth of nonagricultural employment in the late 1970s and early 1980s reflected the disappearance of at least some of these activities, brought about by two sets of forces: growth in demand for labor (primarily male), much of which was stimulated by large increases in government spending in construction and transport; and shifts in both the level of demand for agricultural labor and in the pattern of seasonality, which together generated large increases in agricultural jobs (particularly for women) at certain times of the year.

The obvious question posed by this interpretation is why, if indeed a process of marginalization was underway over much of the 1970s, agricultural wages failed to decline precipitously. This is precisely the same question that arose from the Sukodono evidence and to which the analysis of exclusionary labor arrangements is addressed. The answer is that the reserve labor pool was essentially performing a disciplinary function and that the resurgence of these types of arrangements was made possible by shifts in power relations at the local level, brought about by the New Order.

The analysis of exclusionary arrangements also sheds light on the mechanisms brought into play by changing patterns of seasonality in the late 1970s. Exclusionary institutions like *kedokan* are rapidly rendered less feasible as the peaks of labor demand become sharper and thinner. From the viewpoint of the worker, the ready availability of jobs at certain periods undermines the primary advantage of a *kedokan* contract—job security. Because the worker's opportunity cost is high and rising at precisely the time that the employer requires maximum labor input, *kedokan* is likely to become increasingly ineffective and unattractive as a mechanism of indirect labor management. We would, therefore, expect *kedokan* to vanish as seasonality be-

---

remembered that they do so for different reasons; the landless and small-farm households, as "agricultural deficit" households, must supplement agricultural incomes with relatively open-access occupations requiring little or no capital and offering very low returns. . . . On the other hand, the large-farm and landowning households, as "agricultural surplus" households, are able to invest this surplus in relatively high-capital, high-return activities from which the capital-starved, low-income groups are excluded—rice hullers, pickup trucks, cassava and other processing industries, shopkeeping, "armchair" trading with large amounts of capital, moneylending, etc. (1979: 101) comes more marked, and this is precisely what has happened in some villages (White and Makali 1979; Kasryno et al. 1982).

This analysis also illustrates the dangers of taking wage data at face value in formulating distributional implications. For instance, with intensifying seasonality, a shift from *kedokan* to daily contracts could show up in the aggregate data as rising wages, especially for preharvest tasks.[3] Also, more people will have access to these higher wages. The key point, however, is that the period in which these wages prevail becomes increasingly shorter and the time during which little or no work is available correspondingly longer. Over the course of a year, the total time when there is virtually no agricultural work available will be shortened to the extent that cropping intensity is increasing, but there is a technological limit to such increases in labor demand.

In general, it is important to recognize that shifts in the level and pattern of labor demand are likely to be associated with changes in institutional arrangements that in turn govern who gets access to work and wages; hence the distributional outcomes. Moreover, both the forms of institutional arrangements and the way in which they change can vary tremendously among villages, and our ability to explain these variations is still rudimentary. A clearer understanding of patterns of social control at the local level and their interaction with labor processes would probably shed a great deal of light on these institutional variations.

PROCESSES OF AGRARIAN DIFFERENTIATION AND CLASS FORMATION

Although *kedokan* and other exclusionary arrangements, such as those in Sukodono, are by no means universal, they are extremely important when viewed in terms of agrarian differentiation and class formation. Rather than a simple process of proletarianization, they signify a growing division between

---

3. Precisely how these shifts show up depends on how the macro wage data are constructed. One of the chief problems with these data is that they provide no information on contractual arrangements, and it is therefore impossible to tell how remuneration for contracts like *kedokan* are recorded.

those who are involved in these arrangements and those who are cast into a reserve labor pool.

This divergence from the standard Leninist model is not simply an institutional peculiarity, nor is it particularly useful simply to label it a "transitional form." On a more general theoretical level, it illustrates the limitations of viewing differentiation as a linear process with a rigidly defined set of structural consequences. The flexibility with which supposedly "precapitalist" arrangements disappear and reemerge in response to changing conditions underlines the need for a framework that is helpful in explaining and interpreting the more varied patterns and processes of agrarian change that have been observed in Java, as well as in other countries. In an effort to move in this direction, I shall try now to specify the interconnections and feedback processes among three levels of analysis:

1. Macro political and economic structures, particularly the interests in, and relations with, the rural sector of those in control of the state
2. The structure of relations within rural society and associated modes of labor control
3. Intrahousehold relations and labor deployment.

The key to understanding the distinctive features of agrarian differentiation in Java lies in recognizing that the rural elite is not simply a capitalist class that has emerged in response to technologically determined commercialization. They are in essence a class of favored clients of the state whose opportunities to accumulate hinge in critically important ways on their links with the state apparatus. The general tendency over the course of the New Order regime has been for the state to cater directly to the interests of the rural elite and simultaneously reinforce control over them. Oil revenues have played a critical role in facilitating this strategy.

The processes and mechanisms through which the rural elite have been incorporated into the larger system have in turn created the conditions for changing social relations and modes of labor control within rural society. We have already seen how the militarization of the bureaucracy together with village-level de-

politicization in the early phases of the New Order facilitated
the sudden increase in labor arrangements, such as *kedokan*,
which are structured around exclusionary mechanisms. By un-
covering new opportunities to accumulate for the rural elite,
subsequent shifts in the New Order's agrarian strategy have operated so as to reinforce these processes. In particular, the rural
elite's relationship to supravillage authorities provides them
with preferential access to agricultural inputs and credit and,
perhaps even more important, to a range of highly remunerative nonagricultural activities, such as rice hullers, transportation, and large-scale trade. Moreover, ensuring access to such
opportunities requires the rural elite to invest substantial
amounts of time (and perhaps other resources) in maintaining
these relationships. The lucrative nature of these political and
economic activities raises the opportunity cost of large landowners' time and underlines the importance of a reliable agricultural labor force that can be easily controlled.

Kedokan and other exclusionary arrangements, such as those
in Sukodono, are only one possible set of outcomes, but they
carry far-reaching implications. In the first place, the position
of those who gain access to these more "privileged" labor arrangements diverges significantly from the standard notion of
a rural proletariat. The defining characteristics of these arrangements are the relations of dependency that they engen-
der, which in some instances place the worker in a position of
having actively to identify his or her interests with those of the
employer in nonlabor spheres. Even when this is not the case,
the key that ensures effort is the worker's perception of being
in a relatively privileged position that he or she fears jeopardiz-
ing. A second important feature is that these arrangements
sometimes provide the employer with access to the labor of an
entire household rather than just an individual worker. Thus,
for example, both the sharecropping arrangements in Sukodono and the type of *kedokan* contract that specifies both female
and male tasks operate so as to reproduce the conditions that
drive the "independent" peasant household to the limits of
Chayanovian "self-exploitation" (Chayanov 1966; Mellor
1963).

What about those who are excluded from these arrangements? The situation in Sukodono at the time of the survey was rather atypical in that sugarcane labor was often available in off-peak periods of rice production. Although the poorest households in Sukodono may have been in a rather better position than their counterparts elsewhere in Java, they were engaged in a harsh and unremitting struggle to survive from day to day. These households found themselves in conditions shot through with insecurity, which in turn placed severe constraints on their efforts to gain a livelihood. From the viewpoint of the individual household, the chief source of insecurity was, of course, their restricted access to work and also to credit.

There are two other particularly important sources of insecurity internal to the household that inhibit different households in this group to varying degrees. First, almost all Sukodono households in this excluded group were landless and were therefore almost entirely dependent on foodgrains markets, which, particularly in the early 1970s, were subject to sudden and unpredictable price fluctuations. An important consequence of such dependence is that, in the event that a landless household does have the option of choosing between an activity (or set of activities) that offers potentially high but uncertain returns and one in which the returns are low but assured, the latter is likely to appear more attractive than it would to a household in a more secure position.[4] Thus, the tendency for poorer households to intensify their work effort when levels of remuneration fall is not simply a reflection of the income effect dominating the substitution effect; it also probably reflects what I have elsewhere termed the risk of proximity to subsistence (Hart 1978).

The consequence, of course, is that the household is far less able to undertake the type of activities that hold out at least some possibility of accumulation and upward mobility. There is, however, one possible way out of this trap for households without access to productive assets or to secure employment: being able to raise several children to an age when they can

4. This line of argument was first developed by Lipton (1968).

become actively engaged in income-generating work. The comparatively small group of landless households that managed to do this were in a position to diversify their portfolio of activities in ways that small households and those with a low ratio of income earners to total household members simply could not. Conversely, the most destitute and poverty-stricken households were by and large also the smallest ones—most notably those with female adults or elderly couples. Other research has shown that the poorest households in rural Java often find it extremely difficult, if not impossible, to produce and rear the number of children that they would like (White 1976a), a phenomenon that helps explain the inverse relationship between economic status and fertility (Hull 1976).

It is important to bear in mind, however, that the insecure and vulnerable position in which poor households find themselves is not attributable simply to their lack of control over assets and/or their comparatively unfavorable internal structures. The processes through which they have become marginalized reflect their political powerlessness and inability to organize in order to articulate and protect their interests, as well as aggregate labor market conditions. Similarly, the privileged status of the wealthiest households is defined not only by their control over productive assets, but also by their relationship to the state apparatus.

The importance of viewing the intricacies of domestic economic organization within this larger context is that it enables us to move beyond marvelling at the extreme efficiency with which people allocate their appallingly meager resources to inquire into some of the longer-term implications of patterns of resource allocation. The most important implications of the evidence from Sukodono concern the ways in which internal household strategies are not only shaped by resources and social relations, but also operate so as to reinforce them.

The activities of women and children play a particularly important role in shaping these long-run patterns. A prime example is the way in which women from the wealthiest households devote considerable time and effort to social activities, preparing elaborate meals and so forth. These activities are not simply "consumption": they are essential to the household's maintaining its position in the village hierarchy and to cementing the relationships with supravillage authorities that constitute major avenues of access to resources and power. Paradoxically, of course, the essentially supportive nature of such activities means that these women occupy a far more subordinate position *within* the households than poorer women whose heavy involvement in income-generating activities is essential for the household's survival. However, this particular brand of female autonomy both derives from and is reinforced by poverty.

The best illustration of the way in which the household's long-run prospects are shaped and constrained by its short-run allocative patterns lies in what children do. One of the most important changes taking place in the countryside of Java could well be the efforts by wealthier rural households to educate their children for government jobs. In the case of Sukodono, children's education forms a key element in the organizational strategies of influential households. A powerful differentiating force evident at the time of the survey was the way in which children contributed to the economy of poor households, both by releasing adults and by engaging in income-earning activities from an early age. By preventing poor children from acquiring even a primary education, it seemed as though the imperatives of immediate survival were operating so as to reinforce the larger set of forces that condemned poor people to remain poor. Among my most vivid memories of Sukodono is one of an 8-year-old boy dressed in rags who was busily cutting grass at the side of the path for the family's goat to eat. Standing watching him with bemused detachment was the neatly clad young son of a leading Sukodono family, holding his school lunchbox in one hand and a toy in the other.

Why, if the life of the rural poor in Java is so miserable and their prospects so dim, do they not move to urban areas in search of something better? The answer seems to be that, until fairly recently, migration simply was not an option for many poor rural Javanese households. Through most of the 1970s, migration appears to have been limited primarily to younger, better-educated people from relatively well-off households (Aklilu and Harris 1980). The extent to which the rural poor did migrate seems to have been limited primarily to villages that had close links with an urban broker (*tauke*) (generally from that village) who could provide both housing and access to income opportunities in the so-called informal urban sector (which in practice is highly organized) (Jellinek 1977). The available evidence suggests that much of this migration was of a circular nature, with men cycling in and out of the rural economy on a fairly regular basis (Hugo 1977).

Sukodono belongs to that group of villages (probably quite large) with little in the way of urban contacts. Such migration as did take place was limited to a few young women from poor households who went to Jakarta or Semarang, ostensibly in search of domestic work, but who in all likelihood became prostitutes. Another memory from Sukodono is of a tearful old woman imploring me to find her daughter who had gone off to Jakarta many months before and had not been heard of since.

A second question is why the processes of marginalization at work over much of the 1970s failed to produce an explosion of rural unrest. On the face of it, the mechanisms of exclusion seem bound to generate tensions and resentments; this is precisely what happened in Krawang (Boedhisantoso 1976). There are, however, at least two powerful sets of countervailing forces that could explain why Krawang is a special case. First, the fragmented and precarious basis of livelihood of those who are excluded probably militates against the development of class consciousness and collective action (White and Makali 1979). Second, the extremely tight system of military and bureaucratic controls generally ensures that any such moves are unlikely. What is special about Krawang is the massive seasonal movements of labor into the district, which meant that these controls were more difficult to exercise.

A more complex question is whether the macroeconomic changes that took place in the late 1970s and early 1980s have created conditions more conducive to collective action. As a consequence of the more decentralized patterns of disbursement of Inpres and other grants, new construction jobs were springing up in cities and towns all over Java rather than being concentrated in Jakarta, as was the pattern in the past. Industrial expansion also generated new demand for labor, although this was much more regionally concentrated than construction. A third area in which employment seems to have expanded quite rapidly is transportation, which in turn is associated with a rapid increase in spatial mobility:

> Since the mid-1970s . . . there has been an extraordinary increase in the number of short distance Colts [mini-buses], pick-ups and small trucks and, at the same time, a steady upgrading of rural roads under the *Inpres* scheme. Not only has the cost, frequency and convenience of rural/urban transport improved remarkably since ox-carts, occasional buses and a mass of bicycles were the main forms of transport. The psychic distance between village and city has been shortened even more dramatically. (Dick 1982: 35)

An important feature of these new patterns of employment generation is that they appear to have been differentiated along gender and age lines. Jobs in construction and transportation are predominantly male, and many of the workers in industry are young men and women. Consequently, most of those staying behind in the villages are older women and those with children. Access to agricultural jobs may have expanded somewhat, but such jobs have also become more seasonally concentrated.

These shifts in the levels and patterns of employment were accompanied by a sharp increase in labor unrest (Scherer 1982). Such incidents were, however, almost exclusively urban and industrial phenomena, and the youth of the industrial work force probably constitutes an important part of the explanation for them. Not only are young people more likely to take risks; in addition, they have no direct experience of the 1965–1966 massacres.

Whether these events presage a more broadly based labor movement is highly problematic. One set of arguments is that proletarianization has proceeded apace since the late 1970s, with expanding nonagricultural employment and greater spatial mobility resulting in the "freeing" of labor. In addition, greater seasonality in agricultural production could have led to a decline in exclusionary arrangements and greater homogeneity of the agricultural work force.

As in the first part of the 1970s, however, modes of labor organization and the insecurity of livelihood could continue to form constraints on collective action. For example, though little is known about the system of access to new nonagricultural jobs, there are indications that labor contractors (*calo*) may have played an important role in recruiting, organizing, and disciplining labor (Dick 1982). To the extent that this is so, and that access to these jobs has been restricted, labor relations may be far less impersonal than would appear on the surface and the same types of mechanisms that have been analyzed in this book could have been operating. As far as the agricultural work force is concerned, the sharper pattern of seasonality, which has been responsible for shifts in labor arrangements, could also place constraints on the development of agrarian labor movements. The alternating of slack periods of labor demand with brief but intense labor peaks could bring into play the labor-tying mechanisms analyzed by Bardhan (1979), whereby employers act to ensure an adequate labor force by extending credit to workers in the slack season. The more precarious the slack-season sources of livelihood are, the more effective these arrangements are likely to be in ensuring that the work force is not only adequate, but also quiescent.

In short, it may be misleading to presume that the rapid spread of capitalism will lead automatically and inevitably to the development of working-class consciousness and collective action. On the one hand, there are powerful constraints that derive from the imperatives of livelihood and from the labor process itself. On the other hand, the state continues to exercise tight control, which seems to be becoming more openly militaristic.[5] The more relevant issue is whether this system of control can be sustained. The longer-term consequences of agrarian processes lie not so much in the development of working-class movements as in the undermining of the specific mechanisms through which the state attempts to maintain control over the rural sector.

First, however, it is necessary to make explicit the conceptual and methodological bases of this analysis that distinguish it from the orthodox Leninist interpretation. The chief shortcoming of the standard Leninist model is that it abstracts from

5. Mass killings of alleged criminals during 1983 are documented in various issues of the *Far Eastern Economic Review.*

underlying power structures that are clearly revealed in the labor process.[6] In-depth empirical studies are important because they allow a clearer understanding of the mechanisms through which different groups take advantage of changing economic opportunities and extend or deny them to others. The key to using detailed local-level studies in order to elucidate dynamic processes lies in identifying how these mechanisms are both shaped by and act upon larger forces. Approaching agrarian differentiation in this way sheds light on the varying patterns and processes of agrarian differentiation and on the specific contradictions generated by these processes. In the case of Java, we have seen how the state's efforts to maintain control over the countryside have played a central role in shaping the forms of capitalist development.

THE OIL SLUMP AND AGRARIAN POLICY DILEMMAS

Indonesia's first experience of the slackening world oil market was in early 1982 when she was obliged to cut back production by 15 percent, from 1.5 to 1.3 million barrels per day. At the March 1983 OPEC meeting, this ceiling was maintained, but the oil price fell from $34 to $29 per barrel. The drop in foreign exchange receipts from oil exports in 1982–1983 is estimated at about 17 percent, and the balance of payments deficit at over $6 billion. Projections of government revenues over the next few years differ, but it seems clear that declining oil revenues will require a cutback in government spending and a reconsideration of strategies that are no longer feasible. The urgency of such reconsideration is likely to be all the greater to the extent that elements within the state are concerned with problems of poverty. The concern most often expressed by observers is whether the momentum in employment generation can be sustained, particularly if there are spending cutbacks in *Inpres* and related programs, which have been the source of much of the new employment. In general, there is a growing consensus among many policy advisors that the process of adjustment to shrinking oil revenues will require less government

6. For a related critique of the standard Leninist model, see Lehmann (1982.)

intervention along with increasing reliance on market mechanisms; this is seen as a prerequisite not only for greater efficiency, but also for improved equity.

The arguments for greater market reliance in the rural sector stem from two long-standing criticisms of Indonesian government policy. One is that, despite the spectacular success of rice production, the current rice strategy simply cannot be sustained. The costs of subsidizing fertilizer, water, and credit are extremely high, and the public procurement cost of rice is above its landed international price. What is needed now, it is argued, is for rice and fertilizer prices to reflect more closely their opportunity costs, and for this to be combined with a comprehensive food strategy with greater attention to secondary food crops. The second criticism is directed at the government's growing emphasis on rural cooperatives (the KUDs), which are not only extremely inefficient but also inequitable because the lion's share of the benefits are appropriated by the wealthy few who control the cooperatives. Accordingly, poor groups are likely to be better served by impersonal market mechanisms than by a cooperative system in which the rural elite hold sway. Moreover, in an era of diminishing resources, the scope for "trickle down" within or from the cooperatives is smaller and hence the role of the market in serving the needs of the poor even more important.

In a recent analysis of Indonesian agricultural price policy, Dick points out that getting agricultural prices right is not nearly so straightforward as it may appear on the surface (1982). As far as the rice price is concerned, all indications are that the floor price is an ineffective way of insulating farmers from relatively low consumer prices and that its main effect is probably to pass back some of the benefits to those who gain access to the KUD cooperatives. In contrast, the benefits of the fertilizer subsidy together with massive increases in physical supplies seem to have been widely spread and probably constitute the main source of price incentive for increasing production. Thus, a rise in fertilizer price would not only reduce farm incomes but could also discourage fertilizer use on the nonrice crops that many argue are crucial to an integrated food strategy. Budgetary cutbacks mean that fertilizer subsidies will be almost impossible to maintain, and compensating increases in rice prices are likely to be politically explosive. Hence the questions surrounding agricultural price policy essentially constitute a dilemma: the state is in danger of being enmeshed in expensive agricultural support schemes without the option, as in many developed countries, of financing them with artificially high consumer prices (Dick 1982: 31–32).

I suggest that the agrarian policy dilemmas that the state is now confronting are more deep-seated and multifaceted, and also that the benefits that many claim will flow automatically from a more market-oriented strategy are highly problematic. To identify these current constraints on agrarian strategy, the intent of certain policies and some of their unintended consequences need to be examined. The insights into the mechanisms at work within rural society that have emerged from this book provide the analytical tools for doing so. As in the analysis of changes prior to 1978, the key lies in the peculiar and essentially contradictory position of the rural elite vis-à-vis the state apparatus and how this in turn is linked with the structure of relations among different rural groups.

The first point to note is that, though some of the policies in the post-1979 period suggest a new-found interest in the fate of the rural poor, others embody ongoing concerns with earlier issues and similar ways of dealing with them. In particular, both the cooperatives and changes in village government discussed in chapter 2 reflect an intensification of the state's efforts to exercise political control over the rural elite by maintaining them in a position of dependent clientage. Thus, for example, the KUD cooperatives offer opportunities for accumulation but simultaneously allow the *kecamatan* (subdistrict) authorities to control this process. Analogous examples are the shifts in the structure of village government that strengthen the power of the village head by undermining competing forces within the village and the village head's appointment as the lowest-level government official to ensure his or her subordination to the state machinery.

Just as this strategy is inherently contradictory in that it is geared toward strengthening the rural elite on some fronts and tightening control over them on other fronts, so too it contains the seeds of its own destruction and is indeed the chief source of the constraints that the state is now confronting. Three of these are particularly important. First, because the process through which the rural elite are being bought off underwrites their strategies of accumulation, it operates so as continually to raise the costs of maintaining them as politically docile clients. If oil revenues had continued to grow, this strategy could have been sustained for longer, but there must be a limit to it.

A second consequence is that the mechanisms through which the state has attempted to reinforce its control over the rural elite relieves them of pressures from within rural society. The extent to which social relations become more openly antagonistic in turn generates growing needs for the state to reinforce external controls in order to maintain stability. Although this has probably been by and large an unintended consequence, some may perceive advantages in growing class antagonisms:

> [Asked] whether the radical Muslims would pose a threat to the Golkar-Abri [i.e., political and military] leadership, one prominent analyst says he is not worried. This is because these Muslims tend to be the rural elite and are not likely to tie up with and mobilise those urban and rural poor who may feel themselves to be exploited by the system. (*Far Eastern Economic Review*, March 24, 1983)

A third set of constraints derives from the powerful surge of economic growth set in motion by the second oil boom and reinforced by the policy shifts discussed in chapter 2. Although these forces have not led directly to the development of a broadly based working-class movement, they do seem to have operated so as to break down some of the older barriers to mobility, expand education, and facilitate to some extent the incorporation of previously marginal groups. Accordingly, a return to the earlier strategy of economic neglect of the rural and urban poor may become increasingly infeasible.

When viewed in conjunction with one another, these three constraints constitute the core of the dilemma in which Indonesian policy makers now find themselves. Take, for example, the argument that the system of cooperatives should be dismantled and replaced by greater reliance on market mechanisms. The immediate effects of such a move would be to deprive the rural elite of the benefits to which they have become accustomed, and which have probably played an important role in ensuring that they behave as loyal and docile clients of the state. Particularly in such areas as East Java where most of the landholding elite are orthodox Muslims, it is possible that, with the reduction of such privileges and the control that they represent, the dominant rural groups will become more openly antagonistic toward the state. At the same time, to the extent that the withdrawal of state patronage means that the rural elite are cut off from the security of state protection, they may become more vulnerable to hostility from within village society.

The combined effects of these forces could well be to set in motion some important shifts in political alignments at the local level. One possibility is that the rural elite would move in the direction of trying to mobilize and form alliances with poorer groups, both to increase their bargaining power vis-à-vis the state and to protect themselves from internal hostility. This possibility may seem rather remote, but there is little question that the dismantling of state patronage would bring about a dramatic shift in the exercise of social control at the local level. Accordingly, Indonesian policy makers are likely to regard exhortations for greater market reliance with considerable skepticism. At the same time, to the extent that the pursuit of more egalitarian policies is both a political necessity and constrained by the costs of perpetuating the patronage system that keeps the rural elite in line, policy compromises aimed at sustaining divided interests are likely to become increasingly difficult.

In short, the situation of Indonesian policy makers is not, as many observers imply, that they have a rather irrational predilection for outmoded notions of agrarian cooperation, which they can no longer afford and which the logic of the marketplace must now replace. Instead, they are caught up in a profound dilemma analogous in some ways to the agricultural price policy dilemma: they are enmeshed in an expensive system of political control that is becoming increasingly infeasible and simultaneously generating pressures that require increasing control.

Although resource constraints at the macro level have served to highlight and sharpen the agrarian problems that the state is now confronting, a sudden increase in oil revenues is unlikely to constitute a solution. These problems are a reflection of deep-seated contradictions, which derive from the peculiar history of Javanese rural society and economy and which have been set in motion by the state's efforts both to exercise tight control over rural society and to transform its agrarian productive base. In acting to consolidate its power vis-à-vis the "floating mass" of Javanese villagers, the New Order state has generated in a different guise the very threats that it sought to suppress.

Bibliography

Abey, A., A. Booth, and R. Sundrum. 1981. "Labor Absorption in Indonesian Agriculture." *Bulletin of Indonesian Economic Studies* 17: 36–60.

Aklilu, B., and J. Harris. 1980. "Migration, Employment and Earnings." In Papanek, ed., pp. 121–54.

Alexander, J., and P. Alexander. 1978. "Sugar, Rice and Irrigation in Colonial Java." *Ethnohistory* 25: 207–23.

————. 1979. "Labour Demands and the 'Involution' of Javanese Agriculture." *Social Analysis* 3: 22–44.

————. 1982. "Shared Poverty as Ideology: Agrarian Relationships in Colonial Java." *Man* 17: 597–621.

Anderson, B. 1983. "Old State, New Society: Indonesia's New Order in Historical Perspective." *Journal of Asian Studies* 42: 477–96.

Arndt, H. 1971. "Banking in Hyperinflation and Stabilization." In Glassburner, ed., pp. 359–95.

Arndt, H., and R. Sundrum. 1980. "Employment, Unemployment and Underemployment." *Bulletin of Indonesian Economic Studies* 16: 61–82.

Bardhan, P. 1979. "Wages and Unemployment in a Poor Agrarian Economy: A Theoretical and Empirical Analysis." *Journal of Political Economy* 87: 479–500.

————. 1980. "Interlocking Factor Markets and Development: A Review of Issues." *Oxford Economic Papers* 32: 82–97.

Bardhan, P., and A. Rudra. 1978. "Interlinkage of Land, Labour and Credit Relations: An Analysis of Village Survey Data in East India." *Economic and Political Weekly* 13: 367–84.

————. 1980. "Types of Labour Attachment in Agriculture: Results of a Survey in West Bengal, 1979." *Economic and Political Weekly* 15: 1477–84.

Barnum, H., and L. Squire. 1979. "An Econometric Application of the Theory of the Farm Household." *Journal of Development Economics* 6: 79–102.

Bernsten, R., et al. 1981. "The Development and Diffusion of Rice Varieties in Indonesia." Paper presented at the International Rice Research Conference, Manila, April.

Bhalla, S. 1976. "New Relations of Production in Haryana Agriculture." *Economic and Political Weekly* 11: 423–30.

Bliss, C., and N. Stern. 1978. "Productivity, Wages and Nutrition."
Journal of Development Economics 5: 331–98.

Boedhisantoso. 1976. "Rice Harvesting in the Region (West Java) in
Relation to High Yielding Varieties." Monash University, Centre of
Southeast Asian Studies, Research Paper No. 6.

Booth, A., and P. McCawley, eds. 1981. *The Indonesian Economy During
the Soeharto Era*. Kuala Lumpur: Oxford University Press.

Booth, A., and R. M. Sundrum. 1981. "Income Distribution." In
Booth and McCawley, eds., pp. 181–217.

Braverman, A., and T. Srinavasan. 1981. "Credit and Sharecropping
in Agrarian Societies." *Journal of Development Economics* 9: 289–312.

Braverman, A., and J. Stiglitz. 1982. "Sharecropping and the Inter-
linking of Agrarian Markets." *American Economic Review* 72: 695–
715.

Breman, J. 1980. *The Village on Java and the Early Colonial State*. Rot-
terdam, Erasmus University, Comparative Asian Studies Program
Series, No. 1.

Carey, P. 1981. "Waiting for the *Ratu Adil:* The Javanese Village Community on the Eve of the Java War (1825–1830)." Paper presented
at the Anglo-Dutch Conference on Comparative Colonial History,
Leiden.

Castles, L. 1966. "Notes on the Islamic School at Gontor." *Indonesia* 1:
30–45.

Chayanov, A. 1966. *The Theory of Peasant Economy*. Ed. by D. Thorner,
B. Kerblay, and R. Smith. Homewood, Ill.: American Economic
Association, Translation series. (Orig. publ. 1923.)

Collier, W., et al. 1973. "Recent Changes in Rice Harvesting Methods."
Bulletin of Indonesian Economic Studies 9: 36–45.

———. 1974. "Agricultural Technology and Institutional Change."
Food Research Institute Studies 12: 170–94.

———. 1977. "Income, Employment and Food Systems in Javanese
Coastal Villages." University of Ohio, Center for International
Studies, Southeast Asia Series, No. 44.

———. 1978. "Rural Development and the Decline of Traditional Village Welfare Institutions in Java." Western Economics Association
Conference, Honolulu, June.

———. 1982. "Acceleration of Rural Development in Java." *Bulletin of
Indonesian Economic Studies* 18: 84–101.

Connell, M., and M. Lipton. 1977. *Assessing Village Labour Situations in
Developing Countries*. Delhi: Oxford University Press.

Dapice, D. 1980a. "An Overview of the Indonesian Economy." In Papanek, ed., pp. 3–55.

———. 1980b. "Trends in Income Distribution and Levels of Living." In Papanek, ed., pp. 67–81.

Daroesman, R. 1981. "Survey of Recent Developments." *Bulletin of Indonesian Economic Studies* 17: 1–41.

Dick, H. 1979. "Survey of Recent Developments." *Bulletin of Indonesian Economic Studies* 15: 1–44.

———. 1982. "Survey of Recent Developments." *Bulletin of Indonesian Economic Studies* 18: 1–38.

Donges, J., et al. 1980. "Industrialization in Indonesia." In Papanek, ed., pp. 357–405.

Elson, P. 1978. "The Cultivation System and 'Agricultural Involution.'" Monash University, Centre for Southeast Asian Studies.

Emmerson, D. 1976. *Indonesia's Elite: Political Culture and Cultural Politics*. Ithaca: Cornell University Press.

———. 1978. "The Bureaucracy in Political Context: Weakness in Strength." In K. Jackson and L. Pye, eds., pp. 82–132.

Epstein, S. 1962. *Economic Development and Social Change in South India*. Manchester: Manchester University Press.

Falcon, W., et al. 1984. *The Cassava Economy of Java*. Stanford: Stanford University Press.

Fasseur, C. 1981. "The Cultivation System and Its Impact on the Dutch Colonial Economy and Indigenous Society in Nineteenth Century Java." Leiden. Mimeo.

Feith, H. 1962. *The Decline of Constitutional Democracy in Indonesia*. Ithaca: Cornell University Press.

Fernando, M. 1982. "Peasants and Plantation Economy." Ph.D. dissertation, Monash University.

Folbre, N. 1984. "Household Production in the Philippines: A Non-Neoclassical Approach." *Economic Development and Cultural Change* 32: 303–30.

Franke, R. 1973. "The Green Revolution in a Javanese Village." Ph.D. dissertation, Harvard University.

Furnivall, J. S. 1944. *Netherlands India: A Study of Plural Economy*. New York: Macmillan.

Geertz, C. 1956. "The Development of the Javanese Economy: A Socio-cultural Approach." Massachusetts Institute of Technology, Center for International Studies.

———. 1960. *The Religion of Java*. Chicago: University of Chicago Press.

———. 1963. *Agricultural Involution: The Processes of Ecological Change in Indonesia.* Berkeley and Los Angeles: University of California Press.

—————. 1965. *The Social History of an Indonesian Town.* Cambridge, Mass.: MIT Press.

Geertz, H. 1961. *The Javanese Family.* New York: The Free Press of Glencoe.

Glassburner, B. 1978. Political Economy and the Soeharto Regime." *Bulletin of Indonesian Economic Studies* 14: 24–51.

Glassburner, B., ed. 1971. *The Economy of Indonesia: Selected Readings.* Ithaca: Cornell University Press.

Gordon, A. 1978. "Some Problems of Analyzing Class Relations in Indonesia." *Journal of Contemporary Asia* 8: 210–18.

Handoko, B., et al. 1982. "Technological Change, Productivity and Employment in Indonesian Agriculture." Report of a cooperative project by Gadjah Mada University and Boston University, Center for Asian Development Studies, Boston University.

Hansen, G. 1973. *The Politics and Administration of Rural Development in Indonesia.* University of California, Berkeley, Center for South and Southeast Asian Studies.

Hart, G. 1978. "Labor Allocation Strategies in Rural Javanese Households." Ph.D. dissertation, Cornell University.

—————. 1981. "Patterns of Household Labour Allocation in a Javanese Village." In Binswanger et al., eds., *Rural Household Studies in Asia,* pp. 188–217. Singapore: Singapore University Press.

—————. 1983. "Productivity, Poverty and Population Pressure: Female Labor Deployment in Rice Production in Java and Bangladesh." *American Journal of Agricultural Economics* 66: 1037–42.

—————. Forthcoming. "Interlocking Transactions: Obstacles, Precursors or Instruments of Agrarian Capitalism?" *Journal of Development Economics.*

Hayami, Y., and A. Hafid. 1979. "Rice Harvesting and Welfare in Rural Java." *Bulletin of Indonesian Economic Studies* 15: 94–112.

Hayami, Y., and M. Kikuchi. 1982. *Asian Village Economy at the Crossroads: An Economic Approach to Institutional Change.* Baltimore: Johns Hopkins University Press.

Hugo, G. 1977. "Circular Migration." *Bulletin of Indonesian Economic Studies* 13: 57–66.

Hull, V. 1976. "The Positive Relation Between Economic Class and Family Size in Java." Yogyakarta, Gajah Mada University, Population Institute Report Series, No. 2.

Husken, F. 1979. "Landlords, Sharecroppers and Agricultural Labourers: Changing Labour Relations in Rural Java." *Journal of Contemporary Asia* 9: 140–51.

———. 1981. "Regional Diversity in Javanese Agrarian Development: Variations in the Pattern of Involution." University of Bielefeld, Sociology of Development Research Centre, Working Paper No. 10.

Jackson, K., and L. Pye, eds. 1978. *Political Power and Communications in Indonesia*. Berkeley and Los Angeles: University of California Press.

Jaspan, M. A. 1961. *Social Stratification and Social Mobility in Indonesia: A Trend Report and Annotated Bibliography*. 2d ed. Jakarta: Gunung Agung.

Jay, R. 1969. *Javanese Villagers: Social Relations in Rural Modjokuto*. Cambridge, Mass.: MIT Press.

Jellinek, L. 1977. "The Pondok of Jakarta." *Bulletin of Indonesian Economic Studies* 13: 67–71.

Jones, C. 1983. "The Mobilization of Women's Labor for Cash Crop Production." *American Journal of Agricultural Economics* 65: 1049–54.

Jones, G. 1981. "Labour Force Developments Since 1961." In Booth and McCawley, eds., pp. 218–61.

Kahin, G. 1952. *Nationalism and Revolution in Indonesia*. Ithaca: Cornell University Press.

Kano, H. 1980. "The Economic History of Javanese Rural Society: A Reinterpretation." *The Developing Economies* 17: 3–22.

Kasryno, F., et al. 1982. "Institutional Change and Its Effects on Income Distribution in Rural Areas: Case Studies from Four Villages in West Java, Indonesia." Bogor, Agro-Economic Survey.

Knight, G. 1982. "Capitalism and Commodity Production in Java." In H. Alavi et al., eds., *Capitalism and Colonial Production*, pp. 119–59. London: Croom Helm.

Koentjaraningrat. 1961. "Some Social-Anthropological Observations on Gotong-Rojong Practices in Two Villages of Central Java." Cornell University, Southeast Asia Program, Modern Indonesia Project, Monograph Series.

———. 1967. "Tjelepar: A Village in South Central Java." In Koentjaraningrat, ed., *Villages in Indonesia*, pp. 244–80. Ithaca: Cornell University Press.

Kumar, A. 1980. "The Peasantry and the State on Java: Changes of Relationship, Seventeenth to Nineteenth Centuries." In J. Fox et al., *Indonesia: Australian Perspectives*, pp. 577–600. Canberra: Research School of Pacific Studies.

Lehmann, D. 1982. "After Chayanov and Lenin: New Paths of Agrarian Capitalism." *Journal of Development Economics* 11: 133–61.

Leibenstein, H. 1957. *Economic Backwardness and Economic Growth.* New York: John Wiley & Sons.

Leiserson, M., et al. 1978. *Employment and Income Distribution in Indonesia.* Washington, D.C.: World Bank.

Lenin, V. 1899. *The Development of Capitalism in Russia.* Moscow: Progress Publishers.

Lev, D. 1966. *The Transition to Guided Democracy: Indonesian Politics, 1957–59.* Ithaca: Cornell University, Southeast Asia Program, Modern Indonesia Project.

Lewin, M. 1968. *Russian Peasants and Soviet Power: A Study of Collectivization.* New York: W. W. Norton and Co.

Liddle, W. 1978. "Participation and the Political Parties." In Jackson and Pye, eds., pp. 171–95.

Lipton, M. 1968. "The Theory of the 'Optimising Peasant.'" *Journal of Development Studies* 4: 327–51.

Lluch, C., and D. Mazumdar. 1981. *Wages and Employment in Indonesia.* Washington, D.C.: World Bank.

Lyon, M. 1970. "Bases of Conflict in Rural Java." University of California, Berkeley, Center for South and Southeast Asian Studies, Research Monograph No. 3.

McCawley, P. 1981. "The Growth of the Industrial Sector." In Booth and McCawley, eds., pp. 62–101.

———. 1983. "Survey of Recent Developments." *Bulletin of Indonesian Economic Studies* 19: 1–31.

Mackie, J. 1971. "The Indonesian Economy, 1950–1963." In Glassburner, ed., pp. 16–69.

———. 1983. "Property and Power in New Order Indonesia." Paper prepared for the Association of Asian Studies Annual Conference, San Francisco, March.

McVey, R. 1969. Introduction to *Nationalism, Islam and Marxism.* By Soekarno. Cornell University, Southeast Asia Program, Modern Indonesia Project, Translation Series.

———. 1982. "The *Beamtenstaat* in Indonesia." In B. Anderson and A. Kahin, eds., *Interpreting Indonesian Politics*, pp. 84–91. Cornell University, Southeast Asia Program, Modern Indonesia Project, Interim Reports Series, Publication No. 62.

Marx, K. 1967. *Capital.* Vol. 3. New York: International Publishers.

Mazumdar, D. 1959. "The Marginal Productivity Theory of Wages and Disguised Unemployment." *Review of Economic Studies* 26: 190–97.

Mears, L., and S. Moeljono. 1981. "Food Policy." In Booth and McCawley, eds., pp. 23–61.

Mellor, J. 1963. "The Use and Productivity of Farm Family Labor in the Early Stages of Economic Development." *Journal of Farm Economics* 45: 517–34.

Mitra, P. 1982. "A Theory of Interlinked Rural Transactions." Washington, D.C., World Bank, Development Research Center, Discussion Paper No. 33.

Moertono, S. 1974. "State and Statecraft in Old Java: A Study of the Later Mataram Period, 16th to 19th Century." Cornell University, Southeast Asia Program, Modern Indonesia Project, Monograph No. 43.

Mortimer, R. 1974. *Indonesian Communism Under Sukarno: Ideology and Politics, 1959–1965*. Ithaca: Cornell University Press.

————. 1975. "Strategies of Rural Development in Indonesia: Peasant Mobilization versus Technological Stimulation." Asia Society, Seminar on Peasant Organization in Southest Asia, New York, September.

Mubyarto. 1977. "The Sugar Industry: From Estate to Smallholder Cane Production?" *Bulletin of Indonesian Economic Studies* 13: 29–44.

Myrdal, G. 1967. *Asian Drama*. New York: Pantheon.

Onghokham. 1977. "Social Change in Madiun (East Java) during the Nineteenth Century." Unpublished paper.

Paauw, D. 1979. "Frustrated Labour—Intensive Development: The Case of Indonesia." International Labor Organization, Asian Employment Programme, Working Paper.

Palmer, I. 1977. *The New Rice in Indonesia*. Geneva: United Nations, Research Institute for Social Development.

Papanek, G. 1975. "The Poor of Jakarta." *Economic Development and Cultural Change* 24: 1–27.

————. 1980. "The Effects of Economic Growth and Inflation on Workers' Income." In Papanek, ed., pp. 82–120.

Papanek, G., ed. 1980. *The Indonesian Economy*. New York: Praeger.

Pelzer, K. 1971. "The Agricultural Foundation." In Glassburner, ed., pp. 128–61.

Penny, D., and M. Singarimbun. 1973. "Population and Poverty in Rural Java: Some Economic Arithmetic from Srihardjo." Cornell University, International Development Monograph No. 41.

Republik Indonesia. 1983–84. *Nota Keuangan dan Rancangan Anggaran Pendapatan dan Belanja Negara* (Financial Notes and Plan Estimates of National Income and Expenditure). Jakarta.

Robison, R. "Towards a Class Analysis of the Indonesian Military Bureaucratic State." *Indonesia* 25: 17–39.

———. 1982. "The Transformation of the State in Indonesia." *Bulletin of Concerned Asian Scholars* 14: 48–60.

Rodgers, G. 1975. "Nutritionally Based Wage Determination in the Low-Income Labour Market." *Oxford Economic Papers* 27: 61–81.

Sajogyo. 1974a. "Modernization Without Development in Rural Java." Paper prepared for the Study on Changes in Agrarian Structures, Rome, Food and Agricultural Organization.

———. 1974b. *Usaha Perbaikan Gizi Keluarga* (Efforts to Improve Family Nutrition). Bogor: Institut Pertanian Bogor.

———. 1976. "Pertanian, Landasan Tolak Bagi Pembangunan Bangsa Indonesia" (Agriculture, the Basis of Indonesian National Development). Preface to C. Geertz, *Involusi Pertanian*. Jakarta: Bhrarati, K.A.

———. 1977. "Golongan Miskin dan Partisipasinya Dalam Pembangunan Desa" (The Poor and Their Participation in Village Development). *Prisma*. March.

Saropie, S. 1975. "Tingkat Pendapatan dan Penggunaan Tenaga Kerja Penduduk Desa Pantai" (Income Levels and Labor Use in Coastal Villages). Unpublished paper, Bogor.

Scherer, P. 1982. "Survey of Recent Developments." *Bulletin of Indonesian Economic Studies* 17: 1–34.

Schulte-Nordholt, N. 1978. "Integrated Rural Development—Some Comments Based on the Indonesian Situation." Paper prepared for the Seminar on Rural Development on Indonesia, Carnegie Foundation, Washington, D.C.

Scott, J. 1976. *The Moral Economy of the Peasant: Rebellion and Subsistence in Southeast Asia*. New Haven: Yale University Press.

Short, K. 1979. "Foreign Capital and the State in Indonesia: Some Aspects of Contemporary Imperialism." *Journal of Contemporary Asia* 9: 152–73.

Sinaga, R. 1978. "Implications of Agricultural Mechanization for Employment and Income Distribution." Bogor, Agro-Economic Survey.

Slamet, I. 1968. *De Indonesische Dorpssamenleving* (Indonesian Village Life). Amsterdam, Anthropology-Sociology Center, Working Paper No. 3.

Soentoro. 1973. "Sistim Perburuhan Ngepak-Ngedok di 6 Desa Sampel di Jawa" (The Ngepak-Ngedok Labor System in Six Sample Villages in Java). Bogor, Agro-Economic Survey.

Soentoro et al. 1981. "Land Tenure and Labor Markets in East Java, Indonesia." Bogor, Agro-Economic Survey.

Speare, A. 1981. "Migration Trends." In Booth and McCawley, eds., pp. 284–314.

Stiglitz, J. 1976. "The Efficiency Wage Hypothesis, Surplus Labour and the Distribution of Income in LDC's." *Oxford Economic Papers* 28: 185–207.

Stoft, S. 1982. "Cheat Threat Theory: Techniques for Modeling Involuntary Unemployment." Boston University, Department of Economics, Working Paper No. 82, May.

Stoler, A. 1977a. "Rice Harvesting in Kali Loro." *American Ethnologist* 4: 678–98.

———. 1977b. "Class Structure and Female Autonomy in Rural Java." *Signs* 3: 74–89.

———. 1978. "Garden Use and Household Economy in Rural Java." *Bulletin of Indonesian Economic Studies* 14: 85–101.

Strout, A. 1975. "Agricultural Involution and the Green Revolution on Java." Jakarta, Agro-Economic Survey.

———. 1983. "Recent Trends in Employment." Boston, unpublished paper.

Sundrum, R. 1979. "Income Distribution, 1970–76." *Bulletin of Indonesian Economic Studies* 15: 137–41.

Sutherland, H. 1979. *The Making of a Bureaucratic Elite: The Colonial Transformation of the Javanese Priyayi.* Singapore: Heinemann.

ten Dam, H. 1961. "Cooperation and Social Structure in the Village of Chibodas." In *Indonesian Economics: The Concept of Dualism in Theory and Policy*, pp. 345–82. The Hague: W. van Hoeve Publishers.

Terra, G. 1958. "Farm Systems in Southeast Asia." *Netherlands Journal of Agricultural Science* 6: 157–81.

Thompson, E. P. 1967. "Time, Work Discipline and Industrial Capitalism." *Past and Present* 38: 56–96.

Timmer, P. 1973. "Choice of Technique in Rice Milling in Java." *Bulletin of Indonesian Economic Studies* 9: 57–76.

Utami, W., and J. Ihalauw. 1973. "Some Consequences of Small Farm Size." *Bulletin of Indonesian Economic Studies* 9: 46–56.

Utrecht, E. 1969. "Land Reform in Indonesia." *Bulletin of Indonesian Economic Studies* 5: 71–88.

Van der Kolff, G. 1929. "European Influence on Native Agriculture." In B. Schrieke, ed., *The Effect of Western Influence on Native Civilizations in the Malay Archipelago*, pp. 103–25. Batavia: G. Kolff and Co.

———. 1936. "The Historical Development of Labour Relationships in a Remote Corner of Java as They Apply to the Cultivation of

Rice." New York, Institute of Pacific Relations, International Research Series, Report C.

Van Niel, R. 1964. "The Function of Landrent Under the Cultivation System." *Journal of Asian Studies* 23: 357–75.

———. 1983. "Nineteenth Century Java: Variations on the Theme of Rural Change." Paper prepared for the South East Asia Summer Study Institute Conference, University of Ohio.

Ward, K. 1974. "The 1971 Elections in Indonesia: An East Java Case Study." Monash University, Centre for Southeast Asian Studies.

Weinstein, F. 1976. *Indonesian Foreign Policy and the Dilemma of Dependence*. Ithaca: Cornell University Press.

Wertheim, W. F. 1964. *Indonesian Society in Transition: A Study of Social Change*. The Hague: W. van Hoeve.

———. 1969. "From *Aliran* to Class Struggle in the Countryside of Java." *Pacific Viewpoints* 10: 1–17.

White, B. 1974. "Agricultural Involution: A Critical Note." Bogor, Agro-Economic Survey.

———. 1976a. "Production and Reproduction in a Javanese Village." Ph.D. dissertation, Columbia University.

———. 1976b. "Population, Employment and Involution in a Javanese Village." *Development and Change* 7: 267–90.

———. 1979. "Political Aspects of Poverty, Income Distribution and Their Measurement: Some Examples from Rural Java." *Development and Change* 10: 91–114.

———. 1983. "Agricultural Involution and Its Critics: Twenty Years after Clifford Geertz." The Hague, Institute of Social Studies, Working Paper Series No. 6.

White, B., and Makali. 1979. "Wage Labour and Wage Relations in Javanese Agriculture: Some Preliminary Notes from the Agro-Economic Survey." Agricultural Development Council, Conference on Adjustment Mechanisms of Rural Labor Markets in Developing Areas, Hyderabad, India, August.

White, B., and G. Wiradi. 1979. "Patterns of Land Tenure in the Cimanuk Basin: Some Preliminary Notes." Bogor, Agro-Economic Survey.

Williams, G., and Satoto. 1983. "Sociopolitical Constraints on Primary Health Care: A Case Study from Indonesia." In D. Morley et al., eds., *Practising Health for All*, pp. 208–28. Oxford: Oxford University Press.

Wiradi, G. 1978. "Rural Development and Rural Institutions: A Study of Institutional Changes in West Java." Bogor, Agro-Economic Survey, Rural Dynamics Series No. 6, October.

Index

abangan (commoners), 39

AES. *See* Indonesian Agro-Economic Survey

Age, 9, 108, 109, 110, 205. *See also* Child labor; Children

Agrarian Land Law (1870), 22–23, 33, 36

Agrarian Land Law (1960), 28, 95

Agricultural Involution (Clifford Geertz), xiii, 4, 37

Agricultural sector, statistics on, 58–60, 61, 62, 63, 75. *See also* Rice production; Sugar production

aksi sepihak (unilateral actions) campaign, 28

aliran thesis, 38–39

Anderson, B., 26, 31, 42, 53

asli (indigenous) client capitalists, 55, 57

Asset classes: and consumption, 135, 136, 137, 140; and demographic structures, 108–114; and labor allocation, xiii, 115, 117–120, 123–135; resources of, 138, 139; and seasonality, 141–145, 154–162; in Sukodono, 102–108; and wage rates, 148, 149, 154, 170–173, 184–185. *See also* Elites, rural; Landless class

Assets, productive, 107, 122, 125–126, 144. *See also* Fishponds; Land; Livestock

bangsang. See Gathering

Bardhan, P., 8, 11, 12, 13, 171, 172, 206

Barisan Tani Indonesia (BTI), 28, 40

Baud, Governor-General, 22

bengkok (land use rights), 69–70, 95, 100

Bimas Gotong Royong program, 45–46, 94, 95n7

Boedhisantoso, 188, 195

Bogor, 81

Booth, A., 65

British rule, 21–22

BTI, *See* Barisan Tani Indonesia

Bulog *(Badan Urusan Logistik)*, 47, 48

Bureaucracy: and economic policy, 54, 55; and the military, 42, 194, 199; under New Order, 29, 31, 190; and rural sector, 21, 46, 189, 204; under Sukarno, 25, 30. *See also* Local government

buruh dekat (close laborers), 119, 173

calo (labor contractors), 206

camat (head of subdistrict), 31–32, 47

candak kulak (traders') credit, 48

Capital, investment, 137, 139, 177, 197n2; and New Order policies, 51–55, 57

Capitalism, rural, 5–8, 11, 19, 32, 36, 182, 206, 207

carik (village secretary), 90, 91

Cash crops, 21, 22, 23, 24, 160, 161. *See also* Sugar production

ceblokan. See kedokan

Childcare, 89, 134–135, 156

Child labor: allocation of, xiii, 121, 123, 129, 136, 178; importance of, 15, 201–202; with livestock, 110n18, 119n4, 128; seasonal, 148, 154, 157, 158, 159, 162–63, 164; unpaid, 61, 122

Children: consumption needs of, 103; education of, 113–114, 203; and household demography, 88, 109, 110, 111

Chinese community, 26, 36

Class formation, 2, 36–37, 102, 198–207; causes of, 5, 19, 32; and conflict, 6, 37–40; and New Order, 40–44. *See also* Asset classes; Elites, rural; Landless class

Collier, W., 72

Colonial rule: bureaucracy under, 30; and economic growth, 23–24; and rural sector, 4, 19, 21, 22, 32–37, 42, 50; Sukodono under, 79

Commercialization: and agrarian change, 2, 5, 8, 19; and class forma-

Designer: Betty Gee
Compositor: Graphic Composition, Inc.
Text: $^{11}/_{13}$ Baskerville
Display: Baskerville